LEGGY BLONDE

LEGGY BLONDE

A MEMOIR

Aviva Drescher

G

GALLERY BOOKS

New York   London   Toronto   Sydney   New Delhi

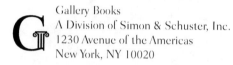

Gallery Books
A Division of Simon & Schuster, Inc.
1230 Avenue of the Americas
New York, NY 10020

First Gallery Books hardcover edition February 2014

GALLERY BOOKS and colophon are registered trademarks of
Simon & Schuster, Inc.

For information about special discounts for bulk purchases,
please contact Simon & Schuster Special Sales at 1-866-506-1949
or business@simonandschuster.com.

The Simon & Schuster Speakers Bureau can bring authors to your live event.
For more information or to book an event contact the Simon & Schuster Speakers
Bureau at 1-866-248-3049 or visit our website at www.simonspeakers.com.

Designed by Akasha Archer

Manufactured in the United States of America

10 9 8 7 6 5 4 3 2 1

Library of Congress Cataloging-in-Publication Data
Drescher, Aviva, 1970–
Leggy blonde: a memoir / Aviva Drescher.—First Gallery Books hardcover edition.
pages cm
1. Drescher, Aviva, 1970—2. Television personalities—United States—Biography. I.
Title. PN1992.4.D65A3 2013
791.4502'8092—dc23
|B|
2013016912

ISBN 978-1-5011-3974-1
ISBN 978-1-4767-2215-3 (ebook)

To my mother

Contents

Preface • 1

Chapter One
It Only Takes a Second • 3

Chapter Two
Flamingo in Manhattan • 27

Chapter Three
Passage in India • 53

Chapter Four
Style on One Leg • 63

Chapter Five
Flamingo Out of Water • 73

Chapter Six
Prune • 89

Chapter Seven
Switch • 107

Chapter Eight
Everything You Wanted to Know about Amputees
(But Were Afraid to Ask) • 121

Chapter Nine
Wild about Harry • 135

CONTENTS

Chapter Ten

Trouble with Harry • 155

Chapter Eleven

It Only Takes a Second, Part Two • 171

Chapter Twelve

My Angel • 187

Chapter Thirteen

My Decade in Court • 199

Chapter Fourteen

Our Modern Family • 217

Chapter Fifteen:

Housewives • 225

Chapter Sixteen

Lost and Found • 239

Acknowledgments • 245

Preface

It's always good for the memoirist to tell a story about the time she almost died." These were the words of advice given to me by a friend when I voiced my trepidation about writing a book.

Good news! I had about five near-death experiences.

Another friend's suggestion: "I like to read memoirs that pull back the curtain on a marriage gone wrong, with all the sordid, destructive lies and details. You know, pain, sadness, heartbreak. Uplifting stuff."

Seduction and betrayal and divorce? I had that covered, too.

A male friend said, "Kinky sex. Something weird. Off the beaten path."

"You mean like, say, amputee sex?" I asked.

"Exactly!"

Um, yeah. Check.

"I'm a junkie for addiction memoirs," said another friend. "Got any substance abuse sagas you can throw in there?"

Unfortunately, yes, I did.

"I'm a sucker for exotic travel stories, like when a normal girl is air-dropped into an upside-down world," said another pal. "I also love weepy hospital scenes, a mother bravely biting back tears next to a kid in an oxygen tent. Oh, and you can't go wrong with dramatic courtroom showdowns, especially if they have a twist ending."

I had plenty of *all* of those stories, actually.

Looking back at my life with newfound objectivity, I realized that it had been a long, unbroken string of wild, one-in-a-million accidents, incidents, and adventures. I hadn't gone looking for any of them, but trouble gravitated toward me. I'd had my share of remarkable good fortune, too. If a person was the sum total of her life experiences, then I was a hell of a lot more than just another leggy blonde.

CHAPTER ONE

It Only Takes a Second

When I was growing up, my parents had a country house in Delaware County in upstate New York near Oneonta. It used to be a barn. From the outside, the building looked pedestrian in this rural setting. But when you entered the house, you entered a world of ultracozy urban sophistication. My parents renovated it into a 1970s-style retreat with shag carpets, a pit fireplace, water beds, and Danish modern furniture. They dug a pond for swimming, and kept a chicken coop. As a child, few things were more gratifying than reaching into the trap door of the hen house and pulling out a still-warm egg. We had pigs and riding horses, and the garage housed a pair of snowmobiles.

My dad, George, was a Jewish kid from Brooklyn, who had become a successful Manhattan accountant. My mom, Ingrid, was German, a child of wartime who had come to America as a teenager and eventually became a model and Pan Am stewardess. She used to joke that he wanted her for the free travel. Dad was rough around the edges, always cursing and usually shocking people. Mom was elegant and refined, a stunning blond classic beauty. She was constantly saying, "Gorsghe!" with the sweetest German accent whenever he was inappropriate. They met when he was sleeping with one of her model roommates. It was love at first sight. By the time Dad told Mom about his wife and three children, she was already hooked. (Dad's first marriage ended soon after. He had three young children, my half-siblings. Barbara, the oldest, lives in Oklahoma and has four children. Michele has one child and lives in New York. Her husband runs the Brotherhood Synagogue on Gramercy Park. Billy is an on-again-off-again drug addict and lives alone in Florida.)

My father's partner in one of his businesses was a man named George Morgan. He lived full time in Delaware County, about fifteen minutes away from our house. The Morgans' wasn't just a country retreat; it was a working dairy farm. Picture cows and horses, rolling grazing hills, a city kid's fantasy of the country.

Dad and George ran tax shelters through some of the local farms. Don't ask me to explain how that all worked. I have no idea. If it sounds a bit shady, that's because it was a bit shady. But back in 1977, it was completely legal.

When I was six, our family moved from our Manhattan apartment to our country house for the summer. It began well, with my dad teaching me to ride a two-wheeler. The final test was to ride down the steep hill and brake at the bottom right before hitting the pond. In typical-me fashion, I went right into the pond, bike and all. Dad ran into the water to save me from drowning (luckily, I had just learned how to swim), and the bike from disappearing in the muck.

One night in June, my parents decided I was old enough for a sleepover at the Morgans' with their daughter Becky. Our families had dinner together at their place, then my parents went home and I stayed. Becky, one of five kids, was seven, and her friend Dawn, who was sleeping over, too, was eleven—which made her four years cooler than Becky. It was one of my first sleepovers. There would be seven kids under one roof, most of them older than me. I was used to nights with my parents and baby brother. This would be a lot more fun.

I don't remember much about the sleepover itself. There was a storm that night but I wasn't scared. It must have been okay, because Becky and Dawn still wanted to hang out with me in the morning. The rain had stopped. It was a perfect blue-sky summer day.

Becky said, "Let's sneak out of the house and ride the barn cleaner in the barn."

Dawn said, "Cool!"

I said, "Cool!" I would have done whatever they wanted. I had no idea what a barn cleaner was, but I liked the sound of "sneak out" and "ride." I threw on jeans, a T-shirt, and my favorite Mickey Mouse sneakers. The sneakers were among my most treasured possessions and I wore them proudly. We ran to the barn, laughing. We jumped in muddy puddles and called them chocolate milk. Becky was barefoot.

The barn had a heavy sliding red door. We went inside and saw a lot of cows. Specifically, a lot of cow *tochis* (Yiddish for behind). The animals were lined up in two rows of about twenty on the left and right sides of the barn. The cows faced the barn wall with their tails toward a center walkway. Positioned right underneath the cows' backsides was an oblong oval made of steel planks inside a metal casing. It reminded me of a baggage carousel at an airport, except this one was multilayered, narrow, and dirty.

Becky flipped a switch right next to the entrance, and the steel oval started moving. It was surprisingly loud, first clanging into operation and then making a grinding sound as it rotated clockwise.

I didn't realize what it was at first. Then a cow lifted her tail, and a cow pie plopped out of her rear end and landed with a wet splat on the barn cleaner. I watched the pile move along the belt until it disappeared through a chute outside the barn; the only sign of the poop when the rotation was complete was a brown smear. I watched with amazement as a few other cows pooped and the belt carried it away, out of sight. The strong smell, though, wasn't going anywhere.

Becky walked all the way down the length of the barn, past the rows of cows, to the back wall, a good two hundred feet from the door. She said, "Just jump on." She showed Dawn and me how to do it. The trick was to get onto the belt with each foot firmly planted on a single plank. The planks shifted underfoot, and if you stepped on the seam, you might fall. Obviously, you didn't want to jump into manure either. I remember having some misgivings about getting my Mickey Mouse sneakers dirty. But I wanted to impress the older girls and prove myself. If they could do it, so would I. Becky rode the belt first. Then Dawn. And then me. Becky did it again and again, each time with a slight refinement, like raising her arms over her head. Dawn would copy her, then me. It was follow the leader.

I was shaky the first few times, but I got the hang of it and thought I was just as good as the older girls. It was almost *too* easy. Becky decided Dawn and I were ready to move on to the next level of difficulty.

"Now we're going to do it on the turn, okay?" she asked, her eyes daring us to chicken out.

By "the turn," she meant the bend in the belt, the U-turn at the door end of the vast barn. I took a closer look at it. When the planks shifted to accommodate the curve, a gap opened farther between them. It was only a few inches wider, but I could see the rusty teeth

6

of the machinery that made the belt go around. The parts looked old, the mechanism primitive. It might've been built a hundred years earlier.

"It's a big deal," said Becky, acknowledging the bravery and skill required for this trick. "It looks easy when I do it, but it's not."

She showed us how. Becky jumped on with expert placement, one foot on each of the two adjacent planks. She held her arms out like airplane wings and leaned slightly forward for balance. The curve seemed to move faster than the straightaway. Her red hair swung as she jumped off, landing on the dirt floor of the barn like a cat. I was really impressed.

Dawn's turn. She copied Becky's style and made it all the way around the turn. When she jumped off, she was laughing. My heart started racing. I wanted to laugh, too, to be part of the crew. I was the youngest, and the smallest, but I could show them that I was just as brave.

My turn.

It didn't go well.

I was supposed to stick the landing but I skidded. Maybe the metal planks were slippery or my Mickey Mouse sneaker treads were worn down or, more likely, I probably just misjudged my jump. I was a clumsy kid—and an even clumsier adult for obvious reasons.

My left foot slid into the gap between the planks. The teeth of the machinery underneath caught hold of it and started pulling my leg down inch by inch. The barn cleaner continued to turn.

I didn't feel pain at first. I just felt stuck and confused about what was happening. There was pressure. I instinctively tried to free myself, but my leg was being pulled down farther into the gap. The pulling and pressure forced me to sit. Then I felt overwhelmed and had to lie back.

The teeth had chewed my leg up to my knee. Becky started to run out of the barn. Dawn, clearly the most intelligent among us, screamed, "Turn it off! Becky, turn it off!" The switch was two hundred feet away. Becky raced down the length of the barn and hit it. The belt ground to a stop and the barn was suddenly quiet—except for, you know, the screaming.

If Dawn hadn't yelled, and if Becky hadn't turned off the belt, I would be dead. The moving steel planks would have chopped my leg off, and I would have bled to death. Even at six, I was aware that I was half an inch away from never seeing my mother again.

Becky and Dawn charged out of there, leaving me alone with the cows. I remember turning my head and noticing a swishing tail and the shape of a hoof. The barn smelled like manure and something new, something metallic, but not metal. It was the iron-rich smell of blood.

Running flat out in a desperate panic, Becky and Dawn reached the Morgans' house in a minute or two. I could hear them screeching for help, their voices shrill and piercing while they ran.

I thought, *Something is really wrong.*

Becky's mother, Linda, rushed through the barn door. I'd always liked her. She was a very nice woman, and the sight of her made me feel better. The sight of me, however, sent her into a wild panic. Whatever Becky told her had not prepared Linda for seeing me ground up to my knee, seeping blood. She tried to pry the steel planks apart, using all her might as she pulled, but they wouldn't budge. Even with the adrenaline strength of the archetypical woman who lifts a car to save an infant trapped underneath, she couldn't move it an inch. I registered how hard she was working, and how important it was for her. Her frustration mounted by the second. She broke out in a sweat and kept talking to me as she worked to free my leg, a rambling commentary that I can't remember a word of. I knew she was doing her best, but I really wanted my mom. I heard a commotion outside the barn. Excited voices, shouts, a siren, and flashing lights—a rescue squad had come.

I passed out.

When I came to, there was a pillow under my head and my father was next to me. He'd been retrieved from his office down the hill. I was glad he was there. I was on my back, and looked up at him as he rubbed my head. Down by my leg, rescue workers were taking apart the barn cleaner piece by piece using blowtorches. I wondered if the blowtorches would burn me. Dark, sticky red was everywhere, on the planks, all over me. Someone had cut off my jeans up to my mid-thigh and put a tight rubber strap around my thigh. The smell of blood was tinny and heavy. People moved in and out of my vision both at frantic speed and in slow motion.

I screamed, loudly and continuously, because I knew what was happening was terrifying. So many adults were freaking out. The pain was, oddly enough, not so bad. It was non-pain. I later learned that I was numb with shock, or had broken through a pain threshold. My brain shut it off. Fear, though, didn't have a threshold.

A man came toward me with a loaded syringe. They were going to give me a shot. From the very first vaccine I can remember getting, like most kids, I'd had a fear of needles. The sight of it then was even more frightening than the blood. I screamed riotously.

"*Stop screaming! Stop screaming! Shut up!*" The man with the needle, sweaty and angry, yelled at me to be quiet. He got right in my face. I was unnerving him, a man trained to keep his cool under the most grisly circumstances.

My father leaned over me and whispered in my ear, "You just keep on screaming, Aviva."

I felt a sting on my arm, and everything went black.

When I woke up the second time, I was still in the barn, on the barn cleaner. Three hours had gone by. It took that long to dismantle the machine. They were only then lifting me out of it. I looked down. My left foot looked like ground meat with bits of shoestring and canvas from my chewed-up Mickey Mouse sneaker mixed in. The pulpy mess hung onto my ankle by a thread and the skin along my shin had been ripped from the bone up to my knee. The bone was denuded, bright white, like a French-cut lamb chop.

A stone wall bordered the property, a common feature of the country farms in that area. As the fields were cleared, the farmer stacked the plowed-up rocks into a wall. That wall was probably older than the house. As I was carried from the barn to the ambulance on a stretcher, I saw people sitting on the wall, dozens of them. The whole town had gathered *Little House on the Prairie* style to wait for the injured child to be rescued. They didn't react when I was taken out; they just silently stared. Years later, I remember watching "Baby Jessica" brought out of the well, and the people cheered and applauded. The Delaware County crowd was somber and subdued. I must have looked pretty bad.

"We're going to the hospital in Albany, Aviva. The doctors will take care of you," said Dad. He was next to my bed in the ambulance. We sped off. The siren blared loudly. I had an IV in my arm and before long, the meds knocked me out.

When I came to for the third time, I was on a steel table in a white room. I was alone, still dressed in my T-shirt and cut-up jeans, no blanket covering me. I looked down and saw the Mickey Mouse sneaker on my right foot. The familiar sight was made grotesque in comparison to my mangled left leg. Grass, hay, and bits of manure stuck to a clump of skin and blood and bone. I burst into tears. My reaction was visceral, a sudden onslaught of hysteria. My foot was destroyed. It was real.

I'd had bumps and bruises before. The sight of blood on a scrape was enough to rattle any six-year-old. This was the same feeling times a million. I was afraid without even understanding what would happen a day, an hour, or a year down the road. I didn't know anything—where I was, where my parents were, what would happen to my leg. All I knew was fear and pain. I screamed wordlessly like a wounded animal.

And then my angel came in.

"Mommy, Mommy, Mommy," I cried and reached for her.

Mom was my everything. I worshipped her. She was truly exquisite. People always said she looked like a Germanic Elizabeth Montgomery from *Bewitched*. She *was* bewitching. When my mom walked into a room, she brought beauty and grace with her. She always smelled wonderful, too. I'd been lying there in that cold, sterile room, wishing for her to appear. And she did. She hugged me and her touch was warm, gentle, and tender.

"Aviva," she said into my hair. It sounded like "Aveeeva" with her accent.

As she held me and said my name, I thought, *Everything is going to be okay*. That's the power of unconditional love. No one else could have comforted me like her, and all it took was one word.

Before leaving the office and arriving at the accident scene, my father called her back at our house. I imagined it like a movie scene: Mom putting flowers in a vase, my baby brother, Andre, then two, playing happily in his wooden high chair, the summer sun streaming in through the kitchen windows. I pictured my German grandmother standing next to Mom at the counter, fixing something sweet and delicious, when the phone on the wall rang. Mom grabs it, untwisting the long cord, and says, "Hello?"

"Ingrid, something terrible has happened," says Dad.

She learns in an instant that her only daughter had suffered a horrific accident. The phone drops in slow motion, hitting the floor with a sonic boom. Our world has blown up. My mother's anguished screams carried across the hills as she collapsed.

When she recovered, Mom drove to Albany and my grandmother stayed behind with my brother.

In that white emergency room, she did her best to calm me down, but I was still hysterical. A nurse or doctor came in. Another needle . . . Another cold steel table. This time, I was naked under a blue surgical blanket and could feel the wheels turning as we rolled down a white corridor.

Surgery Number One: Attempt to Reattach Severed Left Foot

When I next woke up, I immediately vomited. My postop puking soon became a tradition. Every time I woke from surgery, look out. Technicolor yawn.

I felt woozy and was seeing double. The intensive care room vibrated white and bright. It took an hour before the queasiness stopped and I could focus.

My parents were in chairs next to my bed. Dad said, "The doctors reattached your foot." He explained that my foot was fastened to my ankle with sutures and a pigskin wrap. It wasn't a graft. The pigskin served as organic surgical tape, holding it all together. The surgery took fourteen hours, apparently, and was deemed a success, yet I was not out of danger. My foot was bandaged like a mummy, except for my toes sticking out the top.

Every hour, doctors and nurses in white coats came into the room to look at them. The toes were lacking oxygen and blood, dark purple. The doctors pricked them with needles. "Do you feel that? How about this? Do you feel it?" they asked. I didn't feel a thing. My toes were numb. The rest of my leg throbbed and burned unrelentingly.

I stayed in intensive care for a day or two, and then I was wheeled across the hall into another room. I had a roommate, a boy a few years older than me. I had no idea what was wrong with him, and only caught one glimpse before the nurses closed the curtain between our beds. In the middle of the night, I woke up when several doctors entered our room and surrounded the boy's bed. I could see the shadow on the curtain of the doctors holding him down, of his struggling against them. Then I heard the boy's frantic choking and gurgling. They were trying to ram something down his throat. For all I know, the doctors were saving his life, but it sounded like torture. He begged, "Stop!" over and over, his pleas cut off by wet gagging. The doctors weren't swayed by his protest. Whatever they were doing seemed barbaric. I was scared out of my mind that when they finished with the boy, they'd push back the curtain to do the same thing to me.

My parents told me the next day we were leaving Albany and going to Mount Sinai Hospital in New York City, for "more serious medical help," as Dad said. After the night I'd had, quaking in terror about what had happened to the boy, I was ready to get out of there. I would have sprinted to the door, except for my pigskin-wrapped, black Frankenfoot.

My mom and I rode in an ambulance for four hours from Albany to Manhattan. Mount Sinai Hospital was on Madison Avenue and

Ninety-ninth Street, not far from our apartment. I barely knew where I was. City, country, good hospital, bad hospital—I just wanted the hell to end. The ambulance pulled up to the hospital entrance, and my mother's best friend, Sarah, was there to greet us. She was like a godmother to me, and remains a close friend. (Incidentally, Sarah and her sister, along with their husbands, were the cool hippies who created Hotsox, those rainbow toesies tube socks. Remember them?)

My mom beamed at her. "Hi, Sarah!" she said, like it was any other day. Of course, Mom cried and agonized about the accident—for years. But she did it in private. She never let me see her upset. The doctors had been telling my parents all the potential outcomes, including deadly infections and amputation. Mom always managed to keep it light around me. She smiled and tried to raise my spirits. As a mother myself, I marvel at her strength and find myself wondering if she used up her lifetime supply of it that summer, and had nothing left for later on.

Within minutes of settling me into my room at Mount Sinai, the nurses set up an oxygen tent around me, and paid very close attention to my vital signs. Dad demanded it. He took control of the situation and was issuing orders to everyone. His inner Brooklyn tough guy *really* came out when it came to saving his little girl. As a hotshot accountant, Dad worked with some huge names in entertainment and on Wall Street, including Stevie Wonder, the Beatles, Woody Allen, Michael Milken, and the Morgan Stanley banker John Mack, who was also my father's best friend in those days. Dad was the no-bullshit money magician known for saving his clients a ton of cash. By contrast, Mom was gentle and kind, a magnificent shiksa goddess. Together, they were a prominent couple in New York society. When they walked into a room, even a hospital room, they were a force to be reckoned with.

Dad was so well connected he got consultations with every vascular specialist in America and called in the best doctors. Just about everyone he knew tried to figure out how to preserve my leg. He brought in alternative therapists, including a woman who applied fresh aloe sap to my leg to draw out bacteria every hour for a couple of days. A friend of his at the Museum of Natural History unlocked an exhibit to access an ancient sample of some miracle regenerative mineral. Along with the oxygen tent, which was supposed to help blood flow to my foot, I spent hours in a hyperbaric chamber. It looked like a submarine, and mimicked the pressure of descending deep under the sea. My mom went in it with me. It was dark and noisy. A nurse told me that if we ascended too quickly, our skulls would cave in. Naturally, I was terrified of the metal contraption after that.

The traditional doctors were dismissive about the alternative therapy at first, and openly hostile later on. Dad started referring to the doctors as "egotistical moneygrubbing schmucks." This was the beginning of his lifelong loathing and distrust for Western medicine. His frustration with them was a rippling undercurrent of tension throughout my hospital stay.

While Dad tallied up grievances, I collected stuffed animals. Whenever people came for a visit, they brought one for me. I had a hundred piled up behind my bed, and at least five tucked in with me at all times. Letters rolled in from my parents' friends, from rock stars and politicians, who offered to do whatever they could to help. Each new doctor was the great white (and usually Jewish) hope. Dad pulled every string, tried every "cure."

Mom was a loving presence in the chair next to my bed, always smiling and optimistic. They were both desperate to keep me whole and intact. I've since been told that had the accident happened in 2012 and not 1977, reattachment would have worked. The seventies were the infancy of vascular surgery. The chances of saving my foot were none to none.

Cow shit—why in the world did I, or anyone, think playing in manure was fun? Why was that a good idea? Becky suggested we jump around in excrement and I'd said, "Cool!" What the hell was I thinking?

Because of the cow manure infecting my wound, gangrene was running rampant throughout my system. I was put on IV broad spectrum antibiotics. The catheter stayed in my arm for another three weeks.

My toes, meanwhile, went from navy blue to midnight black. The blackness crept from my toes up my foot. It was a week or more before my parents could accept that it would have to go.

They brought in a doctor named Leon Root. (Small world aside: Years later, I went on a blind date with his son, Matt Root. We were having dinner and he mentioned his father was a doctor. I said, "Your father is Leon Root?" Matt nodded. "He consulted on my amputation when I was six!" I announced, a little too enthusiastically . . . probably not ideal small talk on a first date.) Dr. Root had an amazing reputation. He was like a god among mortals. He examined me, then told my parents in the hallway, "The infection is bad. We have to amputate. It's a question of whether we amputate at the knee or the ankle. I recommend the ankle."

That was what my parents wanted to hear. The more leg I had, the more normal my life would be, they thought. They hoped I'd be able to get a screw-on foot of some sort to attach to my leg. Technology advanced every day. Anything was possible in the future, they thought. My father sat down on my bed and told me, "You're going to have another operation. The doctors are going to remove two or three of your toes. You're going to be like the Bionic Woman," he said. I pictured Lindsay Wagner from the hit TV show with her cyber limbs that were ten times stronger and faster than human ones, but was unmoved. I didn't care about having super strength or bionic toes. I didn't care if they chopped off my head at that point. I just wanted the pain to stop. I welcomed surgery. I thought it would be the end of the nightmare.

Surgery Number Two: Amputation of the Left Foot at the Ankle

Another long surgery, another rocky reentry into consciousness. I vomited and waited for my vision to adjust. I knew the operation was to remove my toes, but I could still feel them. I thought, *Guess they didn't take 'em.* The phantom effect—believing you were intact after an amputation—was common. This subconscious trick of the mind brought solace to some, but no one had warned me about it in advance. So when I could see clearly again in my postop haze, I lifted my blanket and looked down at my legs and was genuinely surprised to see that my whole foot was gone. Just leg, and then . . . nothing.

I felt disappointed. I wasn't worried about my ability to walk in that moment. I wasn't picturing myself in a wheelchair, or with a wooden leg like a pirate, or hobbling around with a cane. And I certainly wasn't considering the future and wondering whether or not I'd adapt, fall in love, have children, or lead a relatively "normal" life. My father had looked me in the eye and told me the doctors were taking a few toes. They took the entire foot. I felt lied to.

To this day, Dad and I haven't discussed that day, or that conversation. He was winging it. My parents were in pain in an extraordinary situation that no one could possibly prepare for. They were doing their very best. (Interestingly, they did have some experience in this area. My brother Andre had had a surgery, too. He was born with twelve fingers, and had his extra digits removed surgically at birth. Granted, losing vestigial pinkies was less tense for them than my losing a foot.)

Okay, I thought, *It's really gone. Bummer.* I lowered the blanket and felt a little bit relieved. That surgery marked the end of the wacky treatments. It turned down the dial on my pain. But my hospital stay was only just getting started.

As unsettling as the black desiccated toes had been, they were preferable to a raw stump. Because of the gangrene infection and for other reasons, the surgeons didn't immediately cover my amputation wound with a skin graft. It looked like a science textbook cross section of a leg with the white bone in the middle, surrounded by muscle and ligament.

The wound had to be bandaged tightly and cleaned three times a day. Nurses came into my room to change the gauze and tape. The flesh was raw, and the bandages would stick to the wound and meld into a crust. Every time—and I mean *every single time*—the nurses ripped the bandages off by force, tearing the healing wound open. It hurt more than the teeth of the barn cleaner. As soon as I saw the nurses come into my room with scissors and bandage trays, I would go into hysterics. They had to hold me down. I flailed against them while they unraveled the bandages. It was mayhem.

I didn't—and still don't—understand the wisdom of ripping the flesh open and raw three times a day. Clearly they had their reasons, but as a six-year-old, it struck me as cruel and unusual punishment. My mom used her charm, begging the nurses to come an hour earlier, to mix up their schedule so I didn't fret for an hour in anticipatory dread. She eventually figured out that if she wet the bandages by using a large syringe filled with water, they wouldn't be as sticky. It helped a little. She also tried to distract me by biting my thigh really hard when the nurses changed the bandages.

Once my infection was under control, I was cleared for a skin graft. My parents brought in Victor Rosenberg, a plastic surgeon (renowned for his boob and nose jobs), to talk about how a skin graft could be done. Just as with each surgery and treatment I'd had thus far, my parents and doctors told me that this was the one that would end the misery. The graft was going to make it all okay.

Dr. Rosenberg examined me at the hospital. He was a very lovely, kind man. First, he looked at my stump. Then he turned me over, lifted my gown, and pinched my tush to see if it was fat enough to take skin for the graft.

I was absolutely mortified. A strange man was touching my butt. It was the most embarrassing moment of the entire hospitalization so far. Dozens, maybe hundreds of people had lifted my gown to look at my foot and I didn't care one bit. I'd mentally—and then literally—detached from it. My foot, and then the stump, had become public property in a way. But my butt was still private. Or, it had been. Now even that was under scrutiny.

In the end, as it were, Dr. Rosenberg decided to take skin from my thighs.

Surgery Number Three: Skin Graft to Cover the Base of My Stump

He cut the thigh skin into strips, and arranged it across my stump in a crisscross pattern, like woven dough on top of a pie. The skin graft quickly healed, and the torturous bandage-changing sessions with the Nurses Ratched ended. My pain lessened. For the first time in nearly two months, I wasn't on drugs or in agony. There was a savior, and he came in the form of Dr. Rosenberg.

The pain was reduced so much, I could think about other things. Like love.

While my hospital stay turned my father against medical doctors for the rest of his life, it had the opposite effect on me. I developed a doctor fetish. My first crush was on a resident at Mount Sinai. Whenever he came into my room, my heart would start pounding. I remember him looking a lot like Disney princes, dark wavy hair and piercing blue eyes, bright white smile. He joked around with me, and touched my shoulders to be reassuring. I was almost unbearably excited to see him.

One morning he walked in, happy to see me. I acted like a wise ass, as usual, trying to make him laugh. I was lying on the bed, eating something. Suddenly, he yelled, "Don't eat when you are lying down! Get up! Sit up!" He looked angry and irritated, like I'd broken a rule and proven myself to be a stupid kid.

Obviously, he just didn't want me to choke on my food. The tone was no different than a parent yelling at a child for putting a dry-cleaning bag over her head. I got that. But I'd put all my emotional hunger on him, and when he snapped at me, I felt like I didn't have a friend in the world. As the saying goes, there's a reason it's called a crush.

I had Mom, though. She hardly left my side for the entire two months I spent in the hospital. When she went to the bathroom, she left the door open so I could see her. If not, I would freak. She slept with me, changed my clothes, and gave me sponge baths. When she had to go—to pick up my brother or for whatever reason—her best friends, Sarah and Irena, also a German former Pan Am stewardess, took turns staying with me. They brought me Chinese food from my favorite restaurant, Bruce Ho's Four Seas on Fifty-seventh Street between Park and Lexington (now a Starbucks). Although I loved Sarah and Irena, I cried when they came into my room. Their arrival meant Mom was going to go away. I needed Mom desperately. I couldn't stand to be separated from her. That attachment, and the panic of losing it, I believe, was the basis for the anxiety disorder I later developed.

My dad had to go to work during the day. My two-year-old brother, Andre, was being cared for by my grandmother and baby-sitters. Grandma came to the hospital a few times. My half brother, Billy, Dad's son from a former marriage, came once. A haunted soul, he was sixteen then and already deeply involved with drugs. In the not-too-distant future, he would become a crack addict. That day, though, he was wonderful. He gave me an enormous red panda and told me funny stories for hours. In my experience, the most troubled people are often the sweetest. They carry a certain sensitivity to life's pains and turn to drugs to numb themselves.

At the beginning of August, a team of doctors and nurses crowded into my room. The head nurse cleared her throat to make the announcement. "Aviva is ready to go home," she said. "Congratulations. We'll miss you!"

I appreciated all they'd done for me. My parents had me write thank-you letters to every rescue worker, doctor, and nurse who treated me. But I wouldn't miss any of them for a minute: I was so happy to leave. We didn't have a lot of clothes to pack. I'd been living in hospital gowns for two months. But we did need a second taxi for all of my stuffed animals.

Unbeknownst to me, the original reason we'd moved to the country for the entire summer was so we could renovate, decorate, and move into a new apartment in the city. While I was in the hospital, my dad oversaw the move from our old place into the Kenilworth at 151 Central Park West. The new building was a thirteen-story landmark built in 1903 with a dry moat around the perimeter and a russet brick facade. Along with the historic Dakota, Beresford, and San Remo, the Kenilworth was a perennial on the lists of the most prestigious buildings on the Upper West Side. Our four-thousand-square-foot apartment was on the tenth floor with spectacular views of Central Park from each window.

My dad had grown up on the edge of poverty in Brooklyn, sharing a bed with his grandfather like in *Willy Wonka*. He went from having nothing to wanting for nothing. Now that he had money, he liked to spend it and enjoy it. Our lifestyle was opulent. And this apartment was a major step up from our smaller place on West Fifty-eighth Street. My parents bought it for a mere sixty thousand dollars—even in 1977, that wasn't a lot—because the West Side was considered dangerous compared to the snooty and expensive East Side. In reality, Central Park West was about as dangerous as a pillow fight, but whatever. We felt more at home among the artists and bohemians on the West Side anyway. Our neighbors were Michael Douglas and Bill Moyers. Everyone in the building seemed to have interesting jobs and lifestyles: museum directors, designers, artists, and mavericks.

I rolled into the Kenilworth in a wheelchair for the first time that August. The lobby had high ceilings and marble floors, with architecture and moldings like a European museum. The elevator walls were covered in velvet, with bronze handles and a high, rounded ceiling. Having been cooped up in that small hospital room, it was like leaving a prison for a palace. We took the elevator to our apartment. Excited as I was to explore my lavish new surroundings, I was still too weak to check the place out and went straight to bed to rest.

A day or two later, I got to look around. I noticed that one of the park-facing windows had a big X in tape across it. "What happened here?" I asked.

No one answered me. I found out later that my father had punched the window and broken it. He'd been sleeping in the apartment all summer alone. And when reliving the accident one night, he got livid, had no one to talk him down, and lost control.

Fortunately, our apartment was right above a ledge, so all the broken glass landed on the ledge and not on the street below. But the big blue X remained—a reminder that not everything was perfect.

Otherwise, the place was beautiful. It was photographed for *Architectural Digest* and other magazines. Myron Goldfinger decorated the apartment with wall-to-wall oatmeal-colored carpet, white walls, and floor-to-ceiling mirrors. The dining room was raised on a platform with several steps leading up to a Knoll glass table that seated twelve. The living room was raised, too, with tan leather couches and chairs with chrome arms and legs. My parents' bedroom was huge and their marble bathroom had a giant tub overlooking the park. The shelving throughout the house was custom-made Formica, which was very chic back then. There were also mirrored beams throughout.

The apartment was the ultimate status symbol. The poor German refugee and the Jewish kid from Brooklyn had arrived. I don't know if my parents were analytical about our move coinciding with my accident. In hindsight, it was a fascinating coincidence. The universe gave and it took away, almost simultaneously. It was as if you couldn't have happiness without an equal amount of sadness. We were surrounded by the rich, the beautiful, the famous, the talented—but money and status couldn't protect you from accidents or pain. No one got through life scot-free. Consequently, I have always been skeptical of happy times. Whenever I'm exceeedingly happy, I'm suspicious that dark times are around the corner. It's a mental curse.

Not that any of this mattered to a six-year-old. I just wanted to be a regular kid. I daydreamed about candy and wanted to run around outside in my favorite OshKosh overalls. My parents were ready for normalcy to return as well. But it wasn't instantaneous. I was still weak, and frighteningly pale. I'd gone from staring at the four walls in my old hospital room to being boxed in by the freshly painted white walls of our new apartment. My stuffed animals and I had just moved from one bed to another.

My mom started taking me out in my wheelchair to Central Park. One day we came around a curve in the path, and there was my dad. He was waiting for us, holding a leash with a beautiful, soft, caramel-colored puppy, a sheltie. He handed me her leash. She jumped into my lap, and I hugged her tight. I fell in love in a heartbeat. My parents wouldn't let my brother and me have a pet at our old apartment. I actually recall thinking at the time: *I had to lose the foot to gain a dog?* Not that it mattered. I was so thrilled with her I thought she was worth it. I named my new puppy Clever. We were inseparable from that moment forward.

In late summer, my parents drove me to Roslyn, New York, forty-five minutes away on Long Island, to Lehneis Prosthetics. I was going to get an artificial leg that had a big name attached to it—"prosthesis." The prosthetist, my first of *many*, made a plaster cast of my stump by laying warm wet strips of plaster cloth on my leg. It tickled and my first thought was, *I love this!* Until it dried . . . then the doctor came at me with an electric saw to cut off the cast. When I saw and heard the saw, I had a complete panic attack. I flashed back to the day of the accident for the first time. It's strange, but I hadn't thought of it once in all that time. Meanwhile, the saw itself was tiny and harmless. As soon as the teeth touched skin, it shut off automatically. But the noise triggered the memory. I was traumatized and hysterical. Once again, Mom had to deal with pandemonium and she handled it with that soothing combination of strength and reassurance that had by now become her hallmark.

Summer was coming to an end and I would have to leave the safety of home and return to school without a foot. The prosthesis wasn't ready in September. I was entering second grade, and I'd have to do it on crutches with an exposed stump.

CHAPTER TWO

Flamingo in Manhattan

I went to Ethical Culture, a small private elementary school at 33 Central Park West. I had to wear a sock over my stump and use crutches. I hated it. I didn't want my friends and classmates to gawk at my leg all day. I felt conspicuous and uncomfortable. I just wanted to be one of them, not the freak everyone stared at. The teachers and administrators at Ethical Culture—chiefly, Allan Shedlin, the headmaster—really lived up to the school's name. They handled the situation brilliantly, and any success on my part I owe to the school's community and administration.

In those prehandicap law days, there were no wheelchair-accessible ramps or lifts. The only way into the building was a set of doors at the top of a hundred steps. Scaling those steps on crutches was like climbing Mount Everest. Mom insisted on carrying me at first. I couldn't stand that. But she couldn't stand *not* to do it. It was too painful for her to watch.

My teacher that year, Mr. G, had shaggy hair and round John Lennon glasses, a real urban hippy. Most of the teachers had a similar look. It was a progressive Manhattan school, after all. But Mr. G was a standout. He made the rest of the Kumbaya crew look like Gerald Ford. On the first day of the year, he had all the students in my class sit cross-legged on the floor.

"Let's go around the circle and tell a story about our summer," said Mr. G. "Aviva, why don't you start? Will you tell everyone what happened to you?"

Five seconds into the day, Mr. G dove in—foot first. It was exactly the right thing to do. By putting my stump front and center, the curiosity and questions would be dealt with immediately. I was on the spot, but relieved to get it out in the open. My parents had been in charge of telling the story to doctors and nurses, their friends, and my friends' parents all summer long. This was the first time I'd been responsible for telling the story.

"I was sleeping over a friend's house. We went into a barn and my foot got caught in a machine. I got an infection and had a bunch of surgeries. And now I'm missing part of my foot," I said. I was missing the *entire* foot above the ankle. But I thought it'd be easier for my friends to take the news if they thought I was closer to whole. "I have my leg all the way down to here," I added, touching the end of my stump. "It's all okay. I'm okay."

Intuitively, I knew it was my job to make everyone else feel comfortable. To do that, I had to act like I was completely at ease, like the amputation was no biggie. That was the only way I'd ever be treated like a normal kid.

Mr. G said, "Thank you, Aviva. Who's next?"

And then another kid took his turn to share. The spotlight moved away from me for the first time in months. I had been dreading the first day back, but now that I was sitting in that circle on the floor like every other child in my class, the relief I felt was indescribable.

There was an elevator in the building, the old-fashioned kind with a gate door inside that had to be pulled open and closed manually. The operator was an older black woman and she made it her mission to keep track of my movements. Whenever she saw me, she'd snatch me out of line, bring me to the elevator, and transport me to the cafeteria or art class. She was acting out of kindness. But by singling me out, she foiled my plan. Every time I rode the elevator, everyone was reminded about my foot. I just wanted to take the stairs like the other kids, to keep my place in line. I blamed the crutches as much as the operator's kindness. How could I blend in if I was hobbling around with those damn clunky poles?

My best friend was Joanna. She also lived on Central Park West. Compared to mine, her house was totally traditional. My mom spoke with a German accent, and wouldn't leave the house without perfect clothes, makeup, nails, and hair. My father was constantly cursing, and wore flashy Charvet shirts from Paris and a gold chain with three heads, our names engraved on the back. (You can take the guy out of Brooklyn, but . . . well, you know.) We had a Spanish nanny, a French piano teacher, and German relatives visiting constantly. You'd hear three languages in our kitchen any day of the week.

Joanna's mom, on the other hand, lived in L.L.Bean turtlenecks, jeans, and sneakers, and wore not a drop of makeup. Her hair was short and natural gray. Joanna's dad was a maritime lawyer. He had a mustache and wore khaki pants and navy blazers. My family was ostentatious; Joanna's was understated. I really appreciated the calm at her place, and hung out there a lot.

One afternoon right after the start of school, Joanna and I were playing catch with Slime when some of it got stuck in my hair. As Joanna's mom washed it out, I stood at the sink on my one leg, hopping around and acting goofy. Joanna and her mom cracked up. It was the first time I'd used my leg to make people laugh. Our friendship was sealed. Joanna and I stayed close throughout high school. I have always felt so grateful to her and her mom for making me feel not just normal, but like myself.

"It's here," said Mom when I got home from school one day in November. The prosthesis had finally arrived. I'd gone back and forth to Long Island for fittings several times, but each time, minor adjustments had to be made before I could take it home.

I opened the shipping package, peeled back the wrapping, and there it was. A leg in a box. Well, half a leg. It was a glorious sight, much more exciting than getting a new toy at Christmas. The prosthesis itself wasn't so pretty to look at and certainly didn't resemble an actual human leg. It was a hard, shiny plastic shell in two pieces in an industrial shade of pink. The two pieces opened and closed and fastened with two Velcro straps, one at the top by the knee and one at the bottom by the ankle. The ankle part was as big as an elephant's, as it had to fit over my own bulbous ankle/stump. The "foot" attached at the bottom was a pink Styrofoam oval that looked like an enlarged platypus snout. No toes, no foot shape. Just a rubbery chunk that fit into a shoe. Even in a sock, the foot was weird looking.

The prosthesis wouldn't fool anyone. Even under long pants, the ankle was noticeably large. But it was better than crutches.

I sat right down on the floor and took it out of the box to try it on. With a thick wool sock on my stump, I opened up the two pieces and stuck my leg in. The weight-bearing screws were at the knee, so it was tight there. It was pretty tight all over, actually. I closed the straps and pulled my jeans down over it. I stood up. My balance was off. I favored my good leg, and almost stumbled when I put weight on the fake one. With practice, I'd get used to it. I'd pass for normal.

"You still have to use the crutches with the leg, darling," said Mom, bursting my bubble.

"No, I don't need them."

"Oh, yes you do! If you don't use the crutches, you'll fall down and hurt yourself!"

That was her position. I took the opposing view. I begged and battled with my parents about those hateful crutches. Mom and I had never fought before—feeling angry with her was disturbing enough. Fighting was not our family's style. This was Dad's second marriage. He'd done enough yelling and screaming the first time around. Dad might've been attracted to Mom for her gentle ways and soft voice. They hardly ever disagreed, even during that awful period of our lives.

A lot of people have asked me over the years how the accident affected my parents' relationship. That kind of stress could, and often did, destroy marriages. And they certainly faced down powerful emotions.

Instead of directing their anger at each other, they blamed the Morgans, and sued. I was aware of the lawsuit, but it wasn't openly discussed at home. However, if they had guilt about not being able to protect me or stop my pain, my mother and father didn't dwell on it. They were united in their effort to help me, and shored each other up when treatments failed. Their relationship was strong enough to carry the heavy weight of the accident. As a couple, they were solid. As individuals, however, my mother took it hard. She plastered on her beautiful game face for my sake. Her facade would crack, though, and not before long.

"When you came out of my womb, the first thing I saw were your long, long legs," she used to say when telling the story of my birth.

"They put you on my chest, and I counted your fingers and toes." I imagined her pride and relief that her newborn daughter was intact, and shared some of her physical attributes—long legs, blond hair. Mom relied on her beauty to help her survive. It helped her get out of Germany. It enabled her to become a model and a flight attendant and it caught my father's eye. She associated beauty with security and comfort.

When one of my long legs was cut short, my mother worried about my future. Would men want me? Would they look at my altered body and find beauty? What would I wear? Would I go to school dances? Could I travel or have a career? Could I even hail a cab? I overheard my mom ask Dad one night, "How will she get up in the middle of the night when her baby cries? Will she ever be able to have children?" (I'd been given so many drugs because of the gangrene, my mother was afraid I wouldn't be able to conceive.)

She struggled with anxiety and Dad grappled with anger. He seethed about the accident having been allowed to happen. I hobbled into the kitchen one morning and found Dad at the table, lost in thought, rubbing his head with enough force to leave marks. I asked, "Dad, are you okay?"

"Fine, great," he said, snapping back to real time, acting upbeat. But I knew he'd been in the black hole. He didn't talk about his silent rages, at least not to me. But even at six, I understood their worry and anger. It would have been pathological if they hadn't had those feelings. The only emotion I had was a longing to be just like the other kids. So when Mom gave me a hard time about using my crutches with the prosthesis, I was pissed.

I had to prove her wrong, and spent every moment at home getting used to the prosthesis, clomping up and down the hall until my gait was smooth. Some mornings, I would get to the front door and yell, "Gotta go, good-bye!" as if I were in a hurry and "forget" the crutches. I tried a few times to stick them in the coat closet and sneak into the elevator without them, but I always got caught. It was as bad as getting caught stealing as far as my mom's reaction went. I also complained about Mom's taking me to school every day. Other kids took the bus or walked themselves.

Dad could tell how important all this was for me, and helped convince Mom to loosen the reins. Two against one, we wore her down. Finally, she said, "Okay. You can leave the crutches at home under one condition: Mack will drive you to school, and park outside the building until you get in safely."

Mack was our driver, and a sweet, gregarious ex-con. Imagine a cross between Robert De Niro and Burgess Meredith in *Rocky*. Mack drove our stretch limo. Talk about conspicuous and totally mortifying! I wasn't going to blend in if I was dropped off in a limo. Worse than being thought of as "peg-leg girl" was being tagged a "poor little rich girl." The next morning, I begged Mack to drop me off a few blocks from school. He had clear instructions to take me all the way to school, but I pleaded with him. We compromised. He let me out a block away, and kept an eye on me from the curb. Tight-lipped and determined, I walked to the building by myself and up those one hundred steps. It was exhausting. I had to stop a few times. But I didn't fall down and break my good leg. I made it through the doors in one piece (two, counting the prosthesis).

Victory came at a price. The prosthesis was a step up, but it was functionally flawed. My skin graft at the bottom of my leg was thin, and right on top of the bone. No matter what padding I used—like superthick socks—or how much extra space was built into the lower part of the prosthesis, my skin graft chafed with each step. The first hour in the prosthesis, my graft was abraded raw. In two hours, it was bleeding and open. Often, bone was exposed. But I didn't tell anyone.

My parents asked me a thousand times, "How does the leg feel? Is it comfortable?"

I always said, "Yes!"

Nothing was going to stop me from wearing it. I kept the abrasions a secret for as long as I could, but Mom kept too close a watch. She discovered the problem, and immediately called the prosthetist and my doctors. They tripped a new alarm, which was the last thing either Mom or I needed. Apparently, an open wound by the bone could lead to an infection called osteomyelitis. Unchecked, it could spread rapidly through my entire skeletal system and kill me.

Our reactions to this news were only too predictable.

Mom pretended to be strong, but crumbled in private.

Dad was furious my graft and prosthesis weren't perfect considering what we had all gone through.

I didn't give a shit about the abrasions or osteomyelitis or even the constant pain of walking. Like every other mono- or biped seven-year-old, I cared about vanilla chocolate-chip Häagen-Dazs ice cream, candy, pizza, Disney World, the pictures on my T-shirts, Clever the dog, my stuffed animal collection, Shel Silverstein's *Where the Sidewalk Ends,* and *Star Wars.* I cared about getting the good mat at rest time and the fattest paintbrush in art class. The doctors' warnings were immaterial to me. Scrapes and pain were not going to get in my way. I would have dragged around a leg of solid steel if it brought me a few inches closer to normal.

Mom began her fanatical stump cleaning and disinfecting routine. My prosthesis was refit again and again. The manufacturers tried to use more of a cushion; they designed a larger gap between the stump and the padding; they experimented with reinforcing my knee support. But nothing worked. The abrasions and pain were a part of my daily existence for two decades.

The wounds hurt, but I refused to go to the nurse's office or call home from school. I would just walk through the pain. I would *run* through it. Often, I limped. Whenever I was with children or adults who did not know about the leg, they would ask, "Why are you limping?" The question was innocent, but I would boil inside nonetheless. If someone noticed, it meant I was failing at being normal. I would coolly answer, "I wear a knee brace." There was no way that I was going to explain my whole, heavy story to a stranger.

Pain was the price I had to pay to participate in life. I didn't know why I had to pay it, but I knew I had to. I always marched through it. I would wave at the elevator lady, and then trudge up the stairs. Some days the pain got the better of me by the end of the day. I would get grumpy and often I took it out on my mom.

When I came home from school, I unstrapped the prosthesis and gasped with relief. Mom would come into my room to check the abrasions. If they were particularly bad, she'd excuse herself to go cry in another room. Her game face was starting to falter. Sometimes, if the abrasions were really gross and bloody, she'd dash to the bathroom and vomit. In hindsight, I know now that her secret drinking played a big part in her nausea. But at seven, I had no idea what was really going on with her.

Slowly, surely, my life started to look like a normal second grader's. Obviously, I couldn't do *everything*. But I was able to dance (very important in 1977 when disco was king), roller-skate, and play tag at gym. I lost a lot at running bases. I was glad to lose! It meant I wasn't getting special treatment from the other kids. They were so over my stump anyway. They didn't forget I was missing a foot. But they didn't care. Kids my age were by nature little narcissists—the center of their own worlds. If my leg didn't affect them, they didn't think much about it.

My parents, teachers, and school administrators weren't as blasé. The teachers stealthily kept eyes on me at all times. I learned later about the behind-the-scenes goings-on. My parents requested, and received, hourly updates. They had weekly meetings with school administration. No amount of assurance would have been enough for Mom. If the technology existed back then, she would have texted me a thousand times a day, "R U OK?" Dad was the ringleader of the Monday meetings. They gave him a semblance of control of the unwieldy situation. He couldn't turn back the clock and undo the accident, but he could be vigilant about preventing another. He would have loved to roll me in bubble wrap and lock me in a cushioned room if he could have. Even today he would if he could get away with it. No matter how old we both get, Dad will always think of me as the little girl he told to "keep on screaming."

As a child, I had some awareness that we were well-to-do. I wanted for nothing (except a foot). Not all of our friends and my classmates lived like we did. They didn't fly off to their vacation house for long weekends. They certainly weren't jetting to Africa for spring break. My father was a self-made man. He thoroughly enjoyed his success. Whatever he wanted, he got. Money was no object, whether it was for clothes, cars, houses, art, or food. My parents were so appreciative of all they had since both of them grew up with nothing.

At the Kenilworth, we had an entire hallway of refrigerators, five of them, with glass doors. Why so many fridges? Well, we were a family of four with a household staff of three. My dad had three kids from his previous marriage, and they sometimes lived with us. My mother's relatives visited a lot. Mom had grown up starving in post-WWII Germany. For her, a full fridge meant she was safe and sound. And my father did everything in excess, including stocking the larders.

My parents were fad eaters. When they heard about a trendy diet, they would buy enough of the ingredients and supplements to last for ten years. When my dad read about the *next* diet or secret to long life, they'd get rid of the old stuff and stock up on new supplies as if for a coming ice age. Mom and Dad tried Fit for Life, a regime of elaborate food combining. They'd only eat certain foods, in certain combinations, at certain times. In the end, they couldn't keep up with the plan: they were Fit for Months. Dad read that fresh-squeezed juice was good for you, so he bought an expensive juicer and he drove out to Queens to a wholesaler to buy crates and crates of oranges. Yogurt and wheatgrass raved about by health nuts? Suddenly the fridges were packed with active cultures and the crisper drawers were full of grass, like a square of sod. Wheatgrass juice wasn't available at Whole Foods back then. Whole Foods didn't exist, for that matter. Dad would have to find a guy who sold the stuff—"Got wheatgrass?"—and then do his own juicing.

Diets came and went.

Fashion came and went. Out: Halston and Dior. In: Armani and Donna Karan.

Houses, too. Out: the barn in Delaware County. (A few years after the accident, my parents sold it lock, stock, and barrel. We never went back, and they didn't see the point of holding on to it.) In: The Hammerstein estate (as in Rogers and . . .) in Montego Bay, Jamaica, West Indies. When my dad saw the property, he was instantly smitten. The place was stunning. The estate overlooked the whole island

from the mountains to the sea and had a few individual villas sur-
rounding a pool in the middle. Each villa had its own dining room,
living room, kitchen, and bedrooms. Decorated by John Ryman,
a stylist for Bruce Weber, it had an island oasis vibe, with purple
and coral flowers, four-poster bamboo beds, and enormous plants.
Hummingbirds were everywhere. Design was one of my mother's
passions. She was in heaven working with John, and had another
house featured in *Architectural Digest*.

Why not buy a vacation house in the Hamptons? My father
used to say, "I'm not spending a fortune to just sit in a backyard."
He looked at some impressive estates in Montauk and Sag Harbor,
including the house that Calvin Klein eventually bought on Georgica
Pond in East Hampton. (He kicked himself years later for not buying
that place.) But Dad wasn't a horses-and-luncheon Hamptons kind of
guy. For one thing, it wouldn't be the antidote to city life. Everyone
we knew went to the Hamptons. It was a small, claustrophobic
community. You'd see the same people on the beach as you would on
your block. Dad wanted a true escape—for my sake. In Jamaica, we
had a private pool in a secluded area. I could go swimming and lie
in the sun with my leg comfortably exposed. No one would see me,
stare at me, or pity me.

Buying in Jamaica in 1980 was risky, though. It wasn't very safe
then. A man named Sterling guarded the estate. He was old and sweet,
and carried an automatic rifle. At night, we closed the villa gates and
locked them with five-inch-thick unbreakable padlocks. We would always catch Sterling falling asleep at his post. We all found this hysteri-
cally funny, except for my mother, who said, "What happens if burglars
come in and shoot Sterling while he is asleep?" That was typical Mom.

My parents loved to entertain, and invited friends down to
Jamaica often. If the gates and guards put them off at first, they

stopped caring after smoking some ganja. Our houseman was responsible for the overall working of the estate, as well as getting pot for my parents' guests. (For the record, Mom and Dad did not smoke pot.) One family friend smoked constantly, wake-and-bake style, out of a supersize cardboard tampon applicator. He'd fall asleep with a lit joint. As I got older and knew what was going on, I lay in bed at night, worrying about a house fire. In addition to the guard and houseman, six other people worked in the house, from gardeners to chefs.

We were members of the nearby Round Hill Club. It had a beach and a bar, and we made friends there from all over the world. Some Round Hill fixtures were Ralph Lauren, Paul McCartney, Alec Baldwin, and Kim Basinger. Celebrities didn't faze us. Dad represented so many famous people that we were inured. Before John Lennon was shot, Dad used to go to see him at the Dakota three times a week. Regarding all of his celebrity clients, Dad would say, "Please, Aviva. Their shit stinks, too. Their finger goes through the paper."

"Gorsghe!" Mom yelled in response.

"They just got a lucky break," Dad continued. "Remember that." I was trained at a very young age to be unimpressed by bullshit and fame. Thanks, Dad!

Andre and I hung out with the Lauren kids a lot at Round Hill. Our school vacations were on the same schedule, and we often flew down on the same plane with them. One Christmas break, our family got bumped out of first class. My dad's travel agent booked the seats, but when we checked in, they told us our seats were gone. My father was pissed. We were downgraded and when we boarded the plane, in what were supposed to be our seats sat Ralph Lauren and his family. Dad flipped. He screamed, "Ralph, you paid them off! It's not right!" followed by a stream of cursing. He actually grabbed Ralph's collar. The Brooklyn street guy really came out when you messed with his first-class seats! He calmed down when they came up with two seats for my parents in first class. My brother and I sat in the back.

Years later, I briefly dated Andrew Lauren, Ralph's son. We were in Jamaica, and he asked me to have dinner with his family at their house. I was instantly anxious. What would I wear? Ralph was the king of American fashion. I wore Armani. (Major blonde moment.) I walked into their beautiful elegant home. Ralph kissed me hello and said, "Where did you get such great style?" He knew about my leg, and probably assumed I'd be nervous and insecure. A total mensch, he put me at ease with that one phrase. He couldn't possibly know, however, what was making me really nervous. The couches were white. I had my period. All I could think of was, *What if I leak on Ralph Lauren's white couch?*

At dinner, the subject of my dad's first-class meltdown came up. I apologized on his behalf. Ralph assured me it was an airline mix-up. He never used his name to put anyone out. I believed him. We all laughed about it. Ralph said that the incident was what drove him to buy his own jet. A pissed-off George really was that crazy.

When I was eight years old, I would go to sleepovers at my friend Daisy's house. Seventy-five percent of the time, I wound up calling my parents, crying and asking them to come pick me up. Even though she lived two blocks away, I was homesick. Dad dutifully came to get me each time. Not being able to handle a separation might've been the first sign of my anxiety problems. I trained my parents, and myself, to let fear win. As soon as I felt a pang, I called in the cavalry. Nowadays, the conventional wisdom is to talk an anxious child down and make her stay at the sleepover to habituate her to fear. Removing a child from a stressful situation reinforces the message that she can't handle it.

Well, I sure couldn't. When anxious, I felt like I couldn't breathe. There was a tightening in my chest and throat. A nameless, crushing dread stole the air from my lungs. I thought I was dying. I'd tell my mother that I couldn't breathe. She'd rush me to the doctor, who'd listen to my chest. Since I could actually breathe, the doctor would send us on our way.

Anxiety wasn't a popular diagnosis back in the pre-Zoloft era. People took Valium, but that was for stressed-out, overworked adults. Children were too young to get depressed, feel stress, or suffer from anxiety. Psychopharmacology barely existed then, and if it did, it was for the clinically insane. Of course, nowadays, it's almost too easy for anyone at any age to get a diagnosis and prescription to treat neurological and psychological symptoms. As a diagnosis, anxiety has moved to the top of the list.

Thinking you're suffocating was a known precursor to a panic attack. And yet the word "anxiety" never came up in all those doctors' visits. This went on for three years. And then, at eleven, I had my first full-blown panic attack. It coincided with recognizing my mother's drinking problem. I could hear her vomiting in the bathroom five or six times a day. One day, after she emerged red-eyed and shaky, she called me into the den, asked me to sit down on the couch, and then just stared at me.

I asked, "Mommy, what's wrong?"

She said, "I'm sick."

"Like a cold, or a tummy bug?"

"It's a different kind of sick."

She looked weak and fuzzy, but she didn't have a fever. She was throwing up, but didn't have a stomachache. None of it made sense to me, and that was terrifying. My mom was my everything, and something mysteriously bad was going on with her. I found out later she was taking Antabuse, a pill that makes you violently ill if you drink any alcohol after taking it. It was meant to be a deterrent to prevent drinking, but Mom was more determined than that. Dad seemed upset that she was "sick." More than upset. He acted like her illness was her fault. His anger erupted at night. He wasn't violent, but he was on the edge—his rage was palpable. He'd scream and threaten to throw her out the window if she couldn't stop.

Stop *what*, though? I had no idea.

The day after a particularly menacing late-night fight, my parents sat my brother and me down in our den. "Your mother has a drinking problem," said Dad. I honestly did not understand what a "drinking problem" meant. I thought it meant drinking too many liquids. (Annnnnd . . . another blonde moment.) The tone reminded me of the time he told me I was going to have a few toes removed and I woke up with no foot. I thought he was downplaying the problem.

"She's going away to a treatment center for a few months to get help," he said.

"What treatment center?" I asked.

"Phoenix House. It's in Arizona."

I'd had enough geography to know that Arizona wasn't within driving distance of New York City. Okay, so Dad was *not* downplaying the situation. It was serious.

"Are we going, too?" asked Andre. He was seven.

"We're staying here," he said.

Andre looked crushed. He'd been passed between baby-sitters and relatives during the year following my accident. Mom and Dad had, by necessity, given me so much more attention. He was second born and second fiddle. I couldn't blame him for any resentment he might have for me.

I felt as devastated as my brother to lose Mom to rehab. She wouldn't be home for months? That was a long time for a kid, especially one as needy as I was.

During the family meeting, Mom sat quietly, her hands in her lap, staring at the carpet. She let Dad do all the talking. I wasn't sure if this was all his idea, but she certainly didn't look happy about it. She was resigned. Maybe she thought it was a good idea, or she was just going through the motions to please Dad.

I don't remember exactly how her departure for rehab at Phoenix House went. She must have said good-bye, but I can't recall. It did seem like she was home, and sick. And then she was gone. Disappeared. The house still smelled like her, which underscored her absence. I ached for her.

A few days later, Dad came home with a golden retriever puppy. When I suffered a loss, be it limb or parent, Dad bought a dog. I named her Sandy. Clever had died a year or two earlier.

My anxiety episodes got worse in severity and frequency. If Mom were home, she'd rush me to the doctor. But she wasn't there. Those trips must have been a huge pain in the ass for her, and never amounted to anything but a dismissal by the doctors. My mom was my panacea. My rock. With her gone, I was more vulnerable. When my mother was in Arizona, we relied on our baby-sitter. As cool as Carmen was, though, her attention wasn't remotely comparable to Mom's. She also favored my brother. So I would go to my room, lie down, and struggle to breathe until I could.

A week or so after Mom left, Carmen sent me on an errand to Pioneer Supermarket for milk and bread. It was on Seventy-third Street and Columbus, a five-minute walk from our apartment building. I'd made that walk hundreds of times. The avenue block between Central Park West and Columbus was long, with no stores to populate it, and empty of people that afternoon.

Suddenly, I felt outside of myself and very weird. Nothing specific triggered the sensation. I wasn't reacting to a car horn, a loud noise, or a bolt of lightning. I was fine, and then, in the snap of a finger . . . *not*.

My hands turned clammy, my heart raced, my breathing became rapid and shallow, I broke out in a sweat, and I thought I was going to die. The fight-or-flight reaction hit me full force. My instincts were screaming *run!* I took off at full speed (for me), sprinting to Columbus Avenue, toward stores and pedestrians. Being among people felt better. I put my hands on my knees and bent down. Slowly, my heart quieted. My breaths deepened. The panic passed. I never thought it would pass and I seriously thought I was going to have a heart attack or die.

I got the bread and milk at Pioneer and went home. I didn't tell anyone what happened. I thought I'd gone crazy for two minutes and felt ashamed. Those two minutes felt like an hour. I definitely didn't want anyone else to think I was losing it. Our family had more than enough to deal with.

Since I'd felt better among people, I tried not to be alone for fear of that out-of-body sensation coming back. To this day, I still experience these sensations in certain situations, especially on tiny airplanes. However, at least I know what they are. I've never walked that particular stretch of Seventy-third Street alone since that day thirty-odd years ago. My brain associated the attack with that block. Although I knew there was no connection, I avoided the "scene of the crime" for fear of another attack.

That first anxiety episode led to others, about once a month. An attack came when I least expected it. I was completely at its mercy. When it was over, I was amazed to have survived it. I was equally convinced the next attack was going to kill me or push me over the edge into lunacy. My nightmare vision was that I'd fall on the floor, kicking and screaming, and a crowd of people would gather around me, gawking. Not only did I live in fear of that happening, but I also feared being found out that I'd been having the episodes. I kept them secret, just as I hid the abrasions that could have caused osteomyelitis and might have killed me if left untreated. I didn't want anyone to know. I learned to keep the internal sensations from showing. I might get quiet for a few minutes. But otherwise, I appeared normal. Meanwhile, inside, I was coming undone.

When I was fourteen, I found a book on anxiety at a bookstore and finally had a name for what I'd experienced: panic attacks. I wasn't alone. Other people also had episodes of sudden terror. I was so thrilled! I searched the book for a cause . . . say, for example, a gruesome accident as a young child. The best conclusion I could draw at the time was that I was probably born with a predisposition to anxiety and the accident lowered my baseline. My hospital and surgical history brought on hypochondria. Anxiety and hypochondria fed off each other. I became fearful that something would go horribly wrong with my body and mind. An unexplained bruise had to be leukemia. A headache had to be a brain tumor. I believed that *any* tiny symptom meant I was dying. Mom's mysterious illness, and Dad's obsession with weird food and healers, only reinforced my fears.

My mortality *had* been violently challenged. Most people believe in their own immortality until their early thirties. They do reckless stupid things—drive drunk, smoke, party heavily, do drugs, and have unprotected sex—without worrying about the consequences. When they said, "Nothing's going to happen to me," they meant it. I never had that kind of blind faith. For every kid who was warned, "You'll lose an eye!" how many actually lost the eye? One in a hundred thousand? One in five hundred thousand? How about the kids who were told, "You'll lose a foot!" How many actually lost the foot? One in a million?

Something bad *did* happen to me. I was convinced, *If something else bad is going to happen, it'll happen to me.*

Having your foot chewed off as a child affects a person.

My parents sent me to a shrink to talk about it when I was seven or eight. The therapist asked me to draw the barn and the barn cleaner. Crayons were going to cure me. The shrink badgered me to talk about the accident. I hated the sessions, and complained until my parents let me quit. People have suggested that my anxiety was the result of not dealing emotionally with the accident. My response to that is: bullshit. Unless you've walked a mile in my shoe, you can't judge my behavior.

All I wanted was to move forward with my life. I never grieved for the girl I might've been. I never mourned for the lost part of myself— nor will I. I don't do self-pity.

I was, am, determined to have a great life. Not "a great life, considering." I decided very early on that I could do it all. I could go anywhere and be anything. I wouldn't get mystical or romantic about the tragedy. The accident was not "a blessing in disguise." It was an accident, period. It didn't change the essential me. I loved running around, dressing up, and feeling pretty, on one foot or two. The accident didn't make me philosophical or morose. As a teenager, my biggest annoyance about having one foot was that I couldn't wear high heels, miniskirts, or short shorts to get boys' attention. Some might think that was shallow. I think it made me a normal, healthy girl in New York, which was all I wanted to be.

In seventh grade, I switched to the Fieldston School (the same middle/upper school that followed Ethical Culture). The campus was located in Riverdale, the Bronx. I started taking the bus there with older kids. Greg, an eleventh-grader, was a football player with a tender side. There was something wounded and irresistible about him. He talked to me in the halls. The tiniest attention made me fall madly in love. I planned my life around bumping into him. I'd layer on the eyeliner in the bathroom and giggle with my friends about him. He seemed to enjoy my crush, but it went nowhere.

My next serious crush hit in ninth grade. Mike was a year younger than me, but he looked like he was a grown man. He had dark hair everywhere—arms, legs, back, chest. I was fascinated by his pelts. My celebrity fantasy boyfriend back then was Sylvester Stallone (don't laugh!). Mike was the closest I'd seen to that kind of animal masculinity.

Joanna's parents went away for the weekend once and I convinced her to throw a big football game party at her house. The whole team was coming over, including Mike. I tried on dozens of outfits, my hair tousled, with full makeup. He showed up with his friends. An hour later, Mike was in Joanna's parents' bedroom, making out with the hottest girl in the school. Not me. Her name was Justine. Her parents were best friends with my parents, and I always liked her. They lived in the San Remo, the building next door to ours (home to Dustin Hoffman, Demi Moore and Bruce Willis, Diane Keaton, Steve Martin, and Mary Tyler Moore). I had no reason to, but I felt betrayed. After that night, Justine was my sworn enemy.

I was *devastated*. I vowed never to forgive Mike, *ever*. But a few months later, he asked me out. We went to Pig Heaven, a famous Chinese restaurant on Second Avenue. Just being near him and all his manliness set me atwitter. I reached for my Coke, and it went flying across the table, all over the spare ribs, and into (gasp) his lap. My face flamed bright red. I was mortified. Mike was cool about it, though. Imagine if he had made fun of me instead?

You'd think jealous girls would have whispered behind my back, saying something along the lines of, "Why does he want *her*? She only has one foot." If they did, I wasn't aware of it. In fact, in the high school jungle of survival of the fittest, my leg just wasn't a factor. I wasn't teased or bullied. My attitude was that I wouldn't let my leg stop me from doing or being who I wanted to be. I sent a loud and clear "no biggie" message to my friends and classmates. They picked up on it, and believed it. If they wanted to backstab or gossip about me, they had other reasons to do it. But the leg didn't come up.

It could have gone the other way, though. Kids can be cruel. I give a lot of credit to the Fieldston community. The educators and parents were good people. In Manhattan private school circles, Fieldston was an earthy type of place that nurtured tolerance, acceptance, and diversity. They had a course on ethics that taught compassionate behavior. I certainly reaped the benefits of the high ethical standard there.

For Mike's part, he didn't make me feel self-conscious about my leg—except for one time. Before we'd even kissed, Mike asked Joanna, "Does Aviva take off the fake leg when she sleeps? What about in the shower?" Joanna hesitatingly came to me with his list of questions. She knew I would be mortified. I didn't blame him for idle curiosity. But I hoped he was thinking more about my boobs, and whether I was a good kisser. He soon found out, and must have been pleased. Mike and I wound up staying together for all of high school. I wore his football jacket and felt like the luckiest girl in the world.

I lost my virginity to him at Joanna's house, in her parents' bed. No offense to Mike, but losing it was an all-around unpleasant, crummy experience. We'd fooled around five thousand times by then, and had come close to the act itself. Actually doing it was almost a technicality—a very painful technicality. Mike used a condom. When he took it off, he put it on this little wooden statue behind Joanna's parents' bed. We completely forgot about it and went back to our respective homes. On Sunday evening, Joanna called me.

"My parents came home. I'm standing in their room talking to them. And then I see this used condom on their statue!" she said. One can only guess how Joanna dealt with that one.

It took a while for her to forgive me about that.

By the way, I kept my leg on.

Mike didn't ask to see my stump and I didn't volunteer to show him. With the exception of Joanna, I kept the prosthesis on at sleepovers with my girlfriends, too. It was cumbersome, like wearing a boot, which wasn't comfortable in bed. But I felt very self-conscious when I took it off. With Mike, my whole life centered around feeling and looking pretty for him. No way would I disturb that by revealing my most vulnerable and unattractive part.

Senior year, I was in love and drove myself to school every day with my new driver's license. Anxiety was a hibernating bear all winter and into spring. I got accepted to Vassar College and all academic pressure lifted. I got a bad case of senioritis, nonfatal, and slacked off heavily. The prom was coming up and Mike was taking me. I had a beautiful, chic black sleeveless dress picked out and a pair of suede boots to match. Life was great.

Famous last words.

One day in June, I had to drag myself to gym class. I usually was fine about gym, but that day, I was dreading it for no particular reason. In retrospect, I might've been having a psychic moment. We were playing softball and I was in the outfield standing way, way back there, spacing out. I turned my face up to the sun and closed my eyes.

A ball hit me in my cheek and knocked me off my feet.

I was rushed to the nurse's office, and someone fetched my friend Sarah, who remains one of my best friends to this day. She drove me to the city and we went to the hospital. At the ER, an oral surgeon told me my jaw was broken, and that I'd have to have surgery that night. *Here we go again. . . .*

Surgery Number Four: Jaw Wired Shut

Now, you tell me: Was it really that ridiculous for me to think, *If something weird, random, and freaky is going to happen, it'll happen to me?*

It's not paranoia if it's true, right?

My jaw was wired shut for eight weeks, right through graduation and prom. (When I saw *Mean Girls,* I died when Regina George had to wear a neck and shoulder brace at prom.) I had to drink and eat through a straw. I was already too skinny to begin with, and I lost more weight. I looked like a skeleton in my graduation and prom photos. I could barely speak, and mumbled when necessary. If I had to choose, I'd say not talking was worse than not eating, although I missed both, a lot. It was definitely worse than wearing a prosthesis. Mike put up with a lot during those two months. I can only imagine the jokes in the locker room about how his girlfriend couldn't use her mouth.

My friend Rob calls me "clumsy and long." The irony is that 90 percent of my klutz moments have nothing to do with my prosthesis. And unfortunately I didn't leave my clumsiness behind with adolescence either. On *The Real Housewives of New York City,* there was a scene at my fifth anniversary party when I fell down a short flight of stairs. I stumbled on my *good* foot. Who goes on national TV trying to show the world that she can do whatever everyone else can, and then tumbles down three steps on camera? Luckily, in typical form, Reid literally and metaphorically saved me from that fall.

In my own defense, a photographer said, "Aviva! Look up," right before it happened. I wasn't watching my steps. I tried to recover as gracefully as possible, but I felt foolish. I wound up having to wear a bootie on my right foot—prosthesis on the left—for two weeks. (They should have filmed me walking around like that!) For the rest of the party, my ankle was throbbing. I had to take a seat. I wasn't going to limp into a taxi and leave. The cameras were rolling.

I did take the edge off with a glass of Ramona Singer's Pinot Grigio. I drank it in one gulp. And you know what? It tasted pretty good.

CHAPTER THREE

Passage in India

T his summer," said Dad, "we're going to see a messenger sent by God to save the world. His name is Sai Baba, the modern-day Jesus Christ. We're going to his ashram in India and he's going to grow Aviva's foot back." It was 1985. I was fifteen.

My mother sat next to Dad on the couch in the den while he made this stunning announcement. She'd been sober for three years. If she had any objections to Dad's summer plans, she didn't voice them. She loved him deeply and followed his lead.

Andre, then eleven, said, "Wow, India. Sounds cool." He was a passive follower of my dad's ideas and plans, no matter how kooky.

I was too shocked to speak. I glanced at Mom to make sure I'd heard correctly. She nodded at me. The Jesus Christ of India was going to make my foot grow back? Would it appear in a puff of smoke, or would he pull it out of a hat?

"Don't give me that look, Aviva. Sai Baba is a bona fide miracle worker. It's been documented," said Dad. His eyes glowed with the certainty of a recent convert.

Mom confirmed it. "It's true," she said. "He's the avatar of a healing spirit."

My parents had gone completely off their rockers.

"How long will we be there?" I asked, thinking I could tolerate one of Dad's bizarre schemes for a week, ten days tops.

He said, "A month."

"I don't . . . this sounds kind of . . . I think I'll pass." Go to India and live at an ashram? I wasn't 100 percent sure, but India in July sounded hotter than the furnace of hell. My summer plans had been to hang out with my boyfriend, Mike, in the city or Jamaica. Mike and I were madly, deeply, and passionately in love, as only teenagers could be. The thought of being apart was like tearing off another limb.

"It's not open to discussion. We're going to India to meet Sai Baba," said Dad.

Then came the hard sell. According to what Dad had heard and read, Sathya Sai Baba could:

1. Revive the dead.
2. Cure the sick.
3. Materialize objects like gold rings, precious jewels, statues of Krishna, and a "sacred ash" called *vibhuti*, a holy healing substance made by burning cow dung (as if I needed more cow shit in my life).
4. Spit up a golden "lingam," an egg-shaped symbol of the divine.
5. Be in two places at the same time.
6. Conjure his likeness in fire or in the sky.
7. Create energy clouds.

Dad truly believed that Sai Baba wasn't just a messenger from God, he *was* God. He had a legend and a history of incredible stunts. Allegedly, he'd suffered a heart attack and stroke that paralyzed him, and then he cured himself right on stage before a throng of devotees, in classic "I can walk! It's a miracle!" fashion. His ashram in Puttaparthi attracted hundreds of thousands of people a year just to catch a glimpse of the living god.

Dad showed me a photo. It was the mid-eighties, the height of Big Hair. Sai Baba's afro was the highest and bushiest I'd ever seen. It would have looked great on a Harlem Globetrotter or one of the Jackson Five. He had brown skin, a broad nose, and bulging crazy black eyes. He wore a crossing-guard-orange caftan, buttoned up to his neck and flowing down to his feet. If I saw him hanging out in Central Park, waving his arms around and coughing up golden eggs, I'd think he was on drugs.

"He's got millions of followers from all over the world," said Dad. "Doctors and politicians. Not just the needy and uneducated." That was true. The prime minister of India, scientists, and intellectuals from around the globe swore by his divinity.

The description of this ashram—thousands of sick, desperate Kool-Aid drinkers crammed into a remote village in a Third World country—triggered an instant panic attack. I was convinced the trip would kill me.

By no means was I averse to exotic locales. My parents were travel junkies and took my brother and me on trips through Europe. We rode the Orient Express, and went on safari in Africa. Elephants charged at us at top speed, almost squashing our Jeep. We watched a python catch, kill, and swallow a gazelle whole. The Masai Mara people were fascinated by my leg. They cut me to see if I had human blood in my veins. I loved exploring foreign lands and cultures and was grateful my parents had taken me to the far corners of the world.

But this trip to India wasn't a holiday or a wild adventure. It seemed like the desperate plotting of a delusional man who was forcing me to go along with him against my will. I staged a protest and refused to leave New York. My father put a ton of pressure on me. He made me feel like I had no choice. When I left Mike for the airport, I honestly believed I'd never see him again.

My parents, brother, and I flew seven hours to Paris. My anxiety spiked for the entire flight. By the time we landed at Charles de Gaulle Airport, I felt wrung out. We would spend the night in Paris and then continue to India.

For dinner, we went to a restaurant near Sacré-Coeur. I was on the edge of my emotional control and couldn't eat. Mom tried to force food on me, but I was nauseated. I felt light-headed. My chest was tight. Suddenly, the room went dark.

"I'm going blind!" I screamed.

"For Christ's sake, Aviva, they just dimmed the lights," said Dad.

"What is wrong with her?" Mom added.

It was like that the entire trip. Any twinge meant the worst-case scenario.

The next day, we flew to Bombay. The flight was ten turbulent hours in a jam-packed plane. We landed in a place of abject poverty and human suffering like I'd never imagined. Beggars and garbage everywhere. The smells were indescribable. And this was an industrialized city. This was civilization.

Dad said, "We're almost there!"

We then flew to Bangalore, a vacation spot for Indian residents. From there, we drove deeper into the subcontinent in a rickety, overcrowded bus, down hundreds of miles of patchy "road." Hours went by. It was like driving to the end of the world. Finally, we arrived in Puttaparthi, the village that had been built up around Sai Baba's ashram to cater to the seeking masses. Our bus was one of dozens to arrive that day disgorging the faithful, the needy, and the sick, of all races and ages. The hundreds joined the thousands roaming around the place with a glazed expression, like they'd been hit on the back of the head and weren't sure who they were.

"I can't believe we're here!" my parents said to each other. They were excited, and eager to find our rented apartment and settle in. My brother was nonplussed.

I was miserable, of course.

"Change your attitude, Aviva," Mom said sternly.

"Or it might not work, " Dad chimed in.

"It" was the spontaneous regeneration of human flesh. What the best doctors in New York City could not do with state-of-the-art technology, a self-proclaimed god with a Jimi Hendrix 'fro in India would accomplish with cow dung ash. *But only if I changed my attitude.* Skepticism would jinx it.

I felt like the only sane person for thousands of miles.

Dad rented the finest accommodations available: a single prison cell–like room with a cement floor and one small window. It had four cots and a private bathroom with a toilet and a sink with running water. We brought our own toilet paper. This was the luxury package. In 90 percent of the dorms at the compound, the devotees did their business in a hole in the ground and cleaned their hands in the dirt.

By the way, I wasn't being a First World snobby asshole. I wasn't whining about not being adequately pampered at a five-star resort. I was an anxiety-prone hypochondriac teenager in extreme distress, thousands of miles from home. With every breath, I felt germs entering my lungs. The crowds were tighter and riper than anything I'd seen or smelled on a New York subway. My graft abrasions were open and seeping. The shower water came from a well. In my mind, it was a stream of malaria, aimed right at my face. The public drinking water was literally teeming with bacteria. A single sip would cause violent dysentery. We drank only bottled water. Our food came from a canteen truck. It arrived twice a day to feed thousands of people. The menu options were bread and bread. Sometimes we cooked rice and vegetables in our room, but I was afraid the vegetables weren't clean enough, and didn't dare eat them.

Most of the people there were Indian. We met some Europeans and Americans, too. All races were represented from dozens of countries. However diverse the people, they were all of a certain type—the kind of person who joined a cult. I'd expected to be surrounded by the severely sick. Blind lepers, crooked crones shaking tiny canes—biblical suffering stuff. There certainly were sick people who'd come to be cured. But the devoted, in general, appeared to be healthy—physically. Mentally? They had to have a screw loose.

At 4 a.m., we were roused by bells. We rolled off of our cots, got dressed, and joined the herds heading toward a large communal outdoor area that surrounded the palace where Sai Baba rested (he claimed he didn't need sleep). We walked among concrete buildings, wandering elephants, and throngs of people. Everyone wore saris, including us. We bought some in New York before the trip, and continued to add to our collection in India. My mom loved the fabrics and thought the tunics were beautiful. I missed my jeans.

At the palace, people in wheelchairs were rolled to the front for the predawn gathering. Everyone else sat on the floor. We were really packed in tight. And then we waited. It would take hours for Sai Baba to make his appearance. Then he would walk around the people for about ten minutes. When he finally got over to us, Sai Baba waved his hand in the air. *Vibhuti* appeared in his hand. He sprinkled the ash on us. And then he moved on.

Sometimes he materialized beads and jewelry. He'd lift up his hand, and stones would drip out of it. Once he put his hand in an empty bowl, swirled it around, and it was suddenly full of the holy ash. The people around us would bow, pray, cry, and go nuts when he came near. My father claimed to feel "ebullient" when Sai Baba was near. Mom was excited by the spectacle. I admit to feeling a calming energy when Sai Baba was close. But I wasn't healed or relieved of my anxiety about being there. I certainly didn't regrow my appendage like a salamander.

For a lucky (often wealthy) few, Sai Baba would grant a personal audience. He would take you to his private area and do whatever it was he did back there. Despite Dad's campaigning for over a month, our family was not invited over to Sai Baba's place. Dad didn't want to leave Puttaparthi until we had been. I was losing weight, losing my mind. I fantasized about my bed, hot dog vendors, biking in Central Park, Pioneer grocery store, and of course, my boyfriend. I couldn't stand being away from New York. I cried when I thought about Mike.

"What's wrong with you?" Dad asked. "Why aren't you glad to be here?"

After five weeks in saris (you don't know how sorry), Dad agreed to leave. Although we'd been there for a long time, and had been amply showered with burned cow-shit ash, we weren't healed. My parents' faith was stronger than ever, though. Upon our return to New York, they put up framed pictures of Sai Baba around the house, and kept pots of *vibhuti* around the apartment. The space we called "the gallery"—actually, a home gym—was right outside my bedroom. Mom taped photos of Sai Baba on the StairMaster and treadmill. I saw them whenever I entered or left my room, and felt a stab of resentment each time.

They talked about Sai Baba all the time, not only to each other, but with everyone they knew. Their obsessive devotion—and cult recruitment efforts—drove away some of their friends and a few of Dad's big clients. My parents purchased an apartment at the ashram. They went back a few more times and finally landed that private interview with Sai Baba. He used his sleight-of-hand tricks and made jewelry appear. He gave Mom a necklace, and blessed them. She acted like that necklace was a gift from God. As far as they were concerned, it was.

As hard as the conditions were, the worst part of the experience was my parents' impatience with me—and their having gone off the deep end. They were supposed to be responsible caregivers and protectors. When I complained about my fears or raised a doubt about Sai Baba, Dad didn't want to hear it. The ostensible reason we went to Puttaparthi was to heal me. Back home with all those photos around the house, I realized that my parents lied not only to me, but mostly to themselves. The trip wasn't about me. It was always about them. They used me as an excuse to follow their latest fad, the newest health craze. They dragged me along, knowing how hard it would be for me to stand.

What if I *had* believed them, and in Sai Baba? Imagine how disappointed I would have been not to regrow my missing foot.

A classic rite of passage for any teenager was drawing a distinct line between herself and her parents. I was so dependent on Mom, I might never have managed to separate from her if not for that trip. I can't say I came away from the experience a stronger person, but I had become an individual. I had my own thoughts and opinions. My parents forced me to go to India, but they couldn't change my mind.

As much as it pained me to disagree with them, I took pride in it, too.

A lot of accusations were made about Sai Baba over the years to come, including allegations of sexual abuse. He certainly raked in a massive fortune, and curried political favor in his country. He also built schools and hospitals in the poorest regions in India. Some of his scams have been exposed by documentarians and laughed off by Vegas-style magicians on the Internet. On YouTube, you can see videos of a capsule of compressed ash between Sai Baba's fingers. When he waved his hands around, he opened the capsule. Presto chango, a handful of ash. People have raised the critical question, "If Sai Baba could materialize gold and diamond rings, why did he give them to the rich and powerful instead of directly to the poor?" You know what? If he really could spit up gold, maybe he would have given it to the poor. But he couldn't, obviously. He was a fake whose best magic trick was pulling the wool over intelligent people's eyes.

Over the years, I've checked in with Dad about his faith. "So, do you still believe?" I've asked him.

For a long time, he did. But after decades of willful delusion, Dad finally let his guru go. He'd seen too much to believe in magic tricks by then. Although he'd hoped and prayed that gods really walked among us, in the end, Sai Baba had been a sham. There are some realities faith alone just can't change. Dad was embarrassed about all the money he'd spent, for sure. He mumbled a kind of apology to me about forcing me on that trip. And that was enough for me. We all have our own ways of dealing with loss and with life. If I didn't want anyone judging me, who was I to judge anyone else for their beliefs and coping mechanisms?

CHAPTER FOUR

Style on One Leg

My first style role model was my mom's best friend, Sarah. She was six feet tall, gorgeous, sexy, and dressed with the vibrant palette of a peacock. Her fashion coda was cutting edge. As the saying goes, "Talent can hit a target no one else can hit; genius hits a target no one else can see." Sarah had a kind of style genius. She knew how to make the most of her assets and hide any flaws. I studied her style. She would show up at our apartment in New York or the house in Jamaica in tight scoop-neck dresses, cool jeans and chambray button-down shirts, amazing thick winter sweaters over tights.

In comparison, Mom's style was impeccable. It was classic and elegant, not risqué and sexy. She looked neat and crisp. Picture Catherine Deneuve in *Belle de Jour*, with a little Jackie O. thrown in. Sarah entered a room like a ball of fire. She reeked of sex. In my high school phase of experiencing first love, first sex, and passion,

I aspired to be as cool and sexy as Sarah was. My mother's elegant, classic, timeless style was a look I saved for later in life when I became a mom.

Along with inspiration, Sarah gave me reassurance. Every Christmas, Sarah, her husband, Gary, and their son, Bryce, would come to Jamaica for the holiday. Like her outfits, her compliments were way over the top. "Look at Aviva. She's gorgeous! Look at that body! That tiny waist, those broad shoulders. Does her hair dry like that naturally?" she asked. "Oh, God, she's stunning," she'd go on and on. All afternoon, she'd sing my praises.

It was somewhat embarrassing to have my body dissected by my parents' friends, but my self-esteem was being built. A pioneer in fashion who worked with models all day long found me to be beautiful. The attention made me squirm, but I liked it, too. People weren't averting their eyes or staring at only the part of me that was missing. They were looking at other distinctions.

"Look at Aviva's eyebrows," said Sarah. "She looks just like Brooke Shields." At the time—the early eighties—there was no greater compliment than being compared to Brooke Shields. I looked nothing like her, but it didn't matter. My face—my bushy eyebrows—were the topic of discussion. Not the leg.

Sarah and her cohorts might've been going overboard to puff me up, but I was fine with the inflated compliments. When I looked in the mirror, I saw a scrawny, geeky kid with big teeth, baby giraffe knees, and a bony chest. But Sarah made me feel pretty.

Beauty was an objective measure. I wouldn't dare hold myself up to anyone's beauty standard. Pretty, however, was not a standard. Pretty was a feeling. We all know what it means to feel pretty—and to not feel pretty. Sarah gave me an excellent education by the pool in Jamaica on pretty as an emotion. When I felt it, I stood a little straighter. Self-consciousness about my leg was replaced by a bashful pride. She showed me how to isolate and strengthen that emotional muscle. I developed it as I grew up, using her stylish example.

My number-one aesthetic goal as a kid was to cover my leg. That meant tights, leggings, long pants—and boots. The prosthesis was bulky around my ankle. It looked like I had one elephant ankle and one gazelle. I couldn't wear Nikes. The top part of the shoe came up too high. The only sneakers that fit were Keds, which were babyish and uncool. When I was in third or fourth grade, our family went to London for a vacation. My parents took me to the famous British cobbler John Lobb. He made custom lace-up leather boots for me. The look said "Artful Dodger meets Eliza Doolittle." They were the style of boot Helena Bonham Carter wore at award shows, minus the kitten heel. They were custom made in the finest leather and must have cost a fortune.

I hated them. They were too fancy, and actually called more attention to my ankle than the Keds. My parents insisted I wear them, though. Winter, spring, summer, and fall, I wore those boots. I laced them up for hundreds of days in a row. I was thrilled when they finally started to pinch my right toes and gave me blisters; I could get rid of them.

And shorts: forget it. I refused to wear shorts with the prosthesis. I commend amputees who do. But it wasn't my style. Shorts didn't make me feel pretty. They made me feel awkward and conspicuous. When my prosthesis was exposed, people stared at my leg or started asking questions. Covered up, I blended into a crowd.

Even at summer camp, I wore full-length pants. At age nine, I attended the Belvoir Terrace sleep-away camp. It was a posh all-girls camp in Massachusetts with the best facilities, everything a young girl could hope for. I was homesick and plotted to run away daily. I kept my prosthesis and stump hidden. I slept with my leg on every night and changed in the bathroom alone. It was an uncomfortable, challenging summer. Jeans, boots, and sleeping with a prosthetic on did not help the abrasions or provide any respite from the heat.

I became close to a girl in my bunk named Jessie. One day, she asked me to take my leg off and show her my stump. She actually begged me. I trusted her, so we went into the bathroom. I sat on the toilet seat with the lid down and took off my prosthesis. I expected her to say, "Cool." She was a tomboy. Tomboys don't squirm. Much to my dismay, upon seeing my stump, Jessie screamed, cried, and ran out of the bathroom. On the outside, I shrugged. I went into extreme "no biggie" mode and managed to keep the friendship afloat. Inside, I was rocked. It was a life-defining moment. I would never trust anyone again to see my stump without fearing rejection.

Jessie's reaction reinforced my cover-up obsession. On the soccer field, in the softball dugout, or along the mountain trail, the girl in shorts next to me would look at my jeans and inevitably ask, "Aren't you hot?"

Yes, in Massachusetts in August, I was sweating buckets. But wearing shorts would have really brought the heat.

"I'm fine," I said. "Got any stickers?" At nine, I was skillful at changing an awkward conversation topic.

Swimming publically? My rule was: only in Jamaica. The one time I swam at camp, I had to change into a swimming prosthesis in the bathroom, then rush to the lakeshore. Even at the peak of summer, the lake water was damn cold in the mornings. Other girls took their time submerging to get used to the temperature. I jumped right in so no one could see my leg. Ever jump into a freezing cold lake? Only polar bears would consider that fun.

For three decades, I dreaded warm weather. From May to September, I was a prisoner in my own body. It was partially my own fault, due to my fears and hang-ups. Regardless, I loathed bathing suit season. Other kids counted down the days until summer vacation. I counted the days until fall.

By the time I was sixteen, I was already five foot nine and had really long limbs. Although my arms sometimes made me feel like a monkey, they served me well for high school volleyball. I was the setter and captain of the Fieldston volleyball team. I wore sweatpants instead of little shorts like the other girls on the team. It didn't matter. Playing a sport made me feel good about myself—strong and sexy. The knee pads even covered my bulky knee where the prosthetic was fastened. I connected in a positive way with my body. (Another sport that helped there? Sex.)

Along with my high school physical breakthroughs, I also emerged sartorially. I got really into fashion, and wrested control of my wardrobe from Mom.

Out: Mom's style of tailored, classic, clean lines.

In: dresses with leggings, short, tight tube skirts with leggings, and tapered jeans with zippers at the ankle. I had to leave the zippers undone over my prosthesis though. Parachute pants—like clown pants with a small waist, wide around the hips and tapered at the ankles—were *really* in. I couldn't fit them over my ankle either, so I cut the hem. But I still wore them. I was making adjustments, and making fashion work for me.

Whatever I wore, it was tight, tight, tight. My clothes had to be clingy enough to show my form. I was painfully thin. Anything loose looked like I was fighting my way out of a tent. The popular girls—a.k.a., the girls boys liked—had big boobs and shapely Paula Abdul thighs. I had zero curves. I was more insecure about being skinny than about having one leg. I tried to gain weight, but I just kept growing taller. I outgrew my prosthesis so quickly, I would have to limp for months while a new one was being made.

I can almost hear women thinking, *Yes, how awful it must have been for her, being so tall and thin.* But think back to the skinniest girl in your high school class. The girl who looked like she'd been stretched on a rack. The ostrich girl. Now give that girl a big plastic leg and a limp. Get the picture? Blond hair and bushy eyebrows were not going to mitigate that.

Some girls stuffed their bras with socks. I stuffed my thighs with long underwear. I put on two pairs under my jeans to flesh myself out. Instead of changing in the locker room for gym, I took my sweatpants into the bathroom for privacy. The girls thought I was embarrassed to show my leg. Wrong. I was mortified about the long underwear.

I learned the art, the magic, of misdirection. (Maybe I *had* benefited from my summer with Sai Baba.) I could distract people from my skinniness and my leg with clothes and makeup in overdrive. I went full eighties. Madonna was my fashion hero. I did it all. Layered hair with bows, ripped *Flashdance* tops, leggings, multiple belts, leather jackets, and leg warmers, the one fashion trend that worked to my advantage.

I couldn't wear heels, sadly. I didn't get a high-heel prosthetic until I was twenty-eight. I went as far as I could with flats. When shoe shopping, I wore a sock over my prosthetic. It put the salesperson at ease not to see too much. I would also make some comment like, "I'll put the shoes on myself. Thanks. I wear a leg brace."

Doing it myself was far preferable to letting a salesperson do it.

My mother and I used to pick out some shoes, and then the salesperson would kneel down and attempt to put the shoes on me. He would struggle getting the shoe on my prosthetic foot. Mom would say with sad eyes, "My daughter wears a prosthesis." I wanted to kill her. The kids next to us would stare and I thought I was going to die of embarrassment. For a shoe salesperson, the experience must have been freaky. Probably like a guy taking home a woman he meets in a nightclub only to be surprised by a penis in her panties.

With clothes shopping, my strategy was to find a private fitting room. In communal fitting rooms, like at Bloomingdale's, I'd have a friend guard the door. I learned how to dress and undress at lightning speed. I didn't want my leg to become the center of attention or distract my friends from trying things on. When salespeople noticed my leg, their faces would fall and turn serious. It was like puncturing the fun balloon. I would smile and say, "I wear a knee brace." And everyone would relax. That was more palatable than a missing body part.

My makeup and hair were flawless. My mom was my role model in that regard. The woman didn't go to the grocery store without looking head-to-toe perfect. It was an old-school Germanic trait I think. She never let her appearance slip, not until the last few years of her life. I found it sweetly old-fashioned and fabulous that she always reapplied her makeup before my dad came home from work.

I put it on thick back then: black eyeliner, shiny pale pink lip gloss, I did it all. It was all to look the part of a cool, confident chick. I thought, *Okay, so I don't have a whole body. But every other part of me has to be perfect.* My clothes had to be perfect. My body had to be well groomed. Along with feeling pretty, striving for perfection gave me a sense of control. Other aspects of my life had a life of their own—like the abrasions and my anxiety. But clothes, makeup, and hair were mine to master.

When I was in college, Robert Clergerie platform shoes were hot. *Finally*, I could wear trendy shoes. That summer, I wore pants with them every day, and felt fashionable. A friend—in a miniskirt, which was also the look of the summer—and I stood at a bar one night, waiting for the bartender to take our drink order. She fanned herself, and then pointed at my pants and asked, "Aren't you hot in those?"

I thought, *If someone asks me if I'm hot one more time, I'm going to freak.*

"I'm fine," I'd say.

I saw a look flicker across her face then, as she remembered, *Oh, yeah. Leg.*

The bartender arrived at the nick of time. "What are you drinking?" I asked my friend, always moving the conversation to safer ground.

Friends forget about my leg fairly often, actually. We'd go shopping, they'd pull a tiny skirt or pair of shorts off a rack and say, "You'd look so great in these. With your long le—" Then their eyes would go wide, and they'd sputter an apology. As weird as the moment was, it confirmed that I'd done my job. I'd made them forget.

Nowadays, I wear whatever I like. I prefer opaque tights, not necessarily to cover up, but because they're more fashionable than sheer. When patterned tights were hot, I wore them without problem. No matter what, I try to always look as well put together as I can, even when I'm just running errands (another trait I inherited from my mom). When I feel good in my clothes, I feel good in my head. That has nothing to do with my prosthesis. I believe in doing whatever you can to feel strong, beautiful, and happy. Physical imperfections shouldn't stop anyone from feeling pretty. Ever. In fact, it is the imperfections that are often the most beautiful. It took me until my late thirties to realize that.

In season five of *The Real Housewives of New York City*, I appeared on national TV in a bikini, my leg visible for the entire world to see (the world that watches *The Real Housewives of New York City*, anyway), a clear sign that I, and the aesthetics of my prosthesis, have come a long, long way since summer camp. It took until I was forty years old to fully accept myself. With the cameras rolling, I knew there was no turning back now. My days of passing for "normal" were over. I would never be able to go anywhere again without people knowing about the prosthesis. The leg was out of the closet. And it was a huge relief to wade into the water one inch at a time, just like everyone else.

CHAPTER FIVE

Flamingo Out of Water

When I was in tenth grade, shortly after we came back from India, my mother started drinking again. She'd never been a morning person—Dad was the early riser who had breakfast with me and would make me drink his freshly squeezed orange juice. When she was sober, she'd get up to kiss me good-bye and say, "Have a great day. I love you," before I went to school. When she was drinking, though, she stayed in bed.

In the evenings, she wandered aimlessly from room to room. Dad watched TV in the den. Mom would drift in. She sat down for a minute or two, not talking or paying attention to the show. Then she drifted out. She came into my room, said a few slurred words, and seemed fuzzy. Then she walked out. Sober Mom was purposeful, clear, and reliable. I could count on her. Drunk Mom was a muddled, blurry outline of a person. A dotted line of her movements around the house would look like the flight of a bumblebee, swirling and backtracking.

I came to understand that her patterns weren't as random as I thought. When she drifted out of the den or our rooms, she headed straight for the kitchen to sneak wine. One time, I found her guzzling a bottle while standing at the sink. I grabbed it from her and threw it on the floor. Green glass and red wine went everywhere.

She looked me in the eye and said, "I wasn't drinking it."

Her denial couldn't be shattered, even with the evidence of it on the floor around us.

By seventeen, I was ready to get out of New York. I had lived in Manhattan for my entire life. Like all high school seniors, I needed to put some distance between my family and myself. I didn't want to move hundreds of miles away, just far enough to avoid a casual parental drive-by. My high school grades and scores were solid. For my college application essay, I wrote about Sai Baba. For good measure, I threw in a tape of me playing Chopin's "Fantasy in D minor" on the piano. I was accepted to Vassar, a small liberal arts college in Poughkeepsie, New York, my top choice. It was only eighty-five miles away from Manhattan. If I had to, I could be back home in less than two hours.

My boyfriend, Mike, and I made the wise decision to break up the summer before I left town. He still had to finish his senior year at Fieldston, and I was starting a new life upstate. "Who knows what'll happen?" we said tearfully. "We might get back together someday." I couldn't have imagined a better, sweeter first love—or a smoother breakup—than I'd had with Mike. I thought all of my future boyfriends would be as kind, loving, and patient with me. I envisioned going from one fantastic guy to the next, always being the one to end things or mutually parting ways, until I found my prince.

Boy, did I have a lot to learn.

Vassar was founded in 1861 as a women's college, one of the Seven Sisters, for the female siblings of Ivy League brothers. In 1969, Vassar went coed—on paper, anyway. When I arrived twenty years later, it still seemed like male students were theoretical. The ratio was about three to one female to male. The scarce male students themselves were five to one gay to straight. It seemed as though for every straight male, there were four hundred hard-up women. I exaggerate, but not by much. In such dire circumstances, what could a red-blooded American woman do? I lived with two roommates in the dorm called Strong, a.k.a. the lesbian all-girl dorm. The nickname certainly wasn't *entirely* accurate, judging from my dorm room.

The brochure and tour had charmed me with the brick and ivy-covered buildings. I expected Steinway pianos in each dorm, bookish-yet-stylish *The Group*–type women in smart blazers trotting on horses across the quad. I thought we'd stay up until 3 a.m., debating Camus and Nietzsche in black cashmere turtlenecks while holding lattes in our hands.

Instead, Vassar might as well have been Woodstock. Barefoot hippies tripped around campus with dreads, tie-dye pajama bottoms, and Baja pullovers. Parties centered around pot and "funnels," a plastic funnel duct-taped onto a long plastic tube. The funneler put the tube end in her mouth and knelt on the floor, while her friends poured beer into the funnel. You didn't have to be a physics major to understand the effect of gravity on chugging. Beer careened through the teeth, over the tongue, look out stomach, here it comes. I didn't funnel, but it was entertaining to watch my friends do it. They sure got wasted, which was their goal. Inhaling a carbonated beverage at top speed wasn't my thing. It seemed reckless and kind of stupid. I wasn't into drunken girl-on-girl hookups either. And there was no amount of beer on earth that could make Birkenstocks attractive.

Where were the blazers, lattes, and horses?

My leg was a nonissue. Students from Manhattan who knew about it probably told others, but it was not a cause célebrè. Given my dress code of keeping covered, people forgot, didn't know, and certainly didn't give a crap. There was a pile of weed to smoke! Who cared about some girl's fake leg?

The Manhattan students at Vassar hung out together. We were nicknamed, ironically, the "Beautiful People," or BPs. I was kind of awed to find myself in the circle of BPs, even if the classification was meant as an insult. David Prince was a BP, and legitimately gorgeous. A charismatic New Yorker, he was a born socializer, could work any room, and had already dabbled in party promoting. Even by city standards, he talked, walked, and thought lightning fast. I'd heard about him through friends in the city during high school. He seemed to know everyone, and everyone wanted to know him. He was magnetic. Women and men were drawn to him. He was a force of nature that couldn't be contained. I managed to grab hold of him freshman year.

Enter boyfriend number two.

David's best friend was Alex von Furstenberg, son of Diane. One weekend, Alex and his Swedish girlfriend took David and me to Diane's house in Connecticut. We walked in to find the famous designer cooking dinner in the kitchen in her bare feet. And we sat at stools and talked to her while she chopped vegetables. She looked at me and said in a thick French accent, "Darling, you have a beautifooool baaady."

I said, "Thank you!" I wasn't sure if Alex had told her about my leg, or if she noticed anything. I was covered up in jeans, but she was an expert on the female form and might've picked up on my thick ankle. Regardless, her compliment seemed genuine. I accepted it wholeheartedly.

Later that weekend, Alex did 360s in the mud in my brand-new

Wrangler Sahara Jeep, with all four of us hanging on for dear life. It got stuck and we had to be towed out. Hey, I didn't have to funnel to be reckless and stupid. I had my ways. But alcohol would not be one of them. The children of alcoholics tend to become either heavy drinkers themselves or complete teetotalers. With my anxiety and low weight, even a glass of wine at dinner might make me feel disturbingly out of control.

My original intention at Vassar was to major in drama. Acting and playwriting sounded great. But the major mandatorily included set design and costume-making, which weren't as appealing. At one of my first theater classes, the teacher pointed at me and said, "You are sitting in Meryl Streep's chair." That was the kiss of death. I realized in about five seconds that I was not cut out for drama. So I switched to the next choice on my list: French literature.

During the spring break of my sophomore year, my mother and I went to France, just the two of us. Springtime in Paris with Mom. It was very romantic. We had some fantastic meals and put a few dents in the AmEx. At a store called Chevignon, a salesman came up to offer his help. I was nearly blown off my foot. This guy was a cross between Liam Neeson and Johnny Depp—handsome and *sexy*. His French accent was sublime. Yann was the most devastating man I'd ever met.

He showed me some jackets, and then asked me out. Mom let me have dinner with him one night during the trip. I drooled into my soup du jour just looking at him. But that was it. Nothing happened. I was only twenty, and knew my mother was waiting back at our hotel room. Yann probably thought I was just a cute kid. Also, we had the language barrier. His English was limited to articles of clothing and their prices. My French began and ended with the menu. But we had a wonderful time. I felt very grown up, and deliciously sexy.

The City of Lights turned me on. Paris was splitting its seams with men like Yann. If I could find one who spoke decent English to have dinner with, I'd be happier than a *porc dans la merde*. By then, David and I were done. I'd walked into his room and found him in bed with a girl named Vanessa and that was that. Also, Vassar's grunge culture had lost much of its limited charm by then. So I campaigned for my parents to let me move to Paris for the summer.

"I'm a French literature major," I said. "I need language immersion. It'll be great for my academic career."

My parents were all for it. They loved travel, and wanted me to have adventures and be happy. I suspected Mom liked the idea because I'd be one less person in the apartment on the hunt for her stashed wine bottles. The thought gave me a second of misgiving. But then I got over it. I was twenty, and over the moon about living by myself. Compared to the suffocation of Vassar and New York's tight web of social connections, Paris was wide open. No one knew me, or my history, there.

I rented an apartment in the neighborhood called Le Marais in the Jewish quarter on Place de Thorigny right next door to the Picasso Museum. Le Marais was one of the trendier, artsy arrondissements, known for its galleries, clubs—gay and straight—and restaurants. It was the Greenwich Village of Paris. I felt like I'd found my true home. I loved New York, but Paris was . . . *Paris*! It was heart-stoppingly beautiful. Every street, every building, every woman had untouchable style. The cobblestone streets were a little hard to navigate, but I got used to it. Even the cart food was mouthwatering. No boiled hot dogs and greasy knishes here. The vendors sold falafels with hummus or fresh crepes or *jambon et brie* sandwiches, all delicious. A simple omelet, baguette, and coffee was a transcendent meal at the corner bistro. How did they *do* it? I could not leave at summer's end. No way.

Vassar had a junior year abroad program. I applied to study literature in Paris for both semesters, and was approved. My Marais rental
was up. I had to find a new place to live. My friend Samantha Kluge
had a two-bedroom apartment with Eiffel Tower views on Avenue
Emile Zola in the 16th arrondissement. It was *really* expensive, but
my parents let me take it anyway.

My parents contributed. They had me on a Paris budget. But I
had a lot of my own money. When I turned eighteen, I gained access
to the settlement paid to me by the Morgans' insurance company.
I called it my blood money. It was a lot, and I spent freely. I do not
know how much my parents supported me or how much I supported
myself. My father dealt with the finances. I do know that I felt finan-
cially very secure.

The French school program was called Via Paris, for Americans
to immerse themselves in the language and learn about literature
and culture. I took the Metro there and back, roamed around the
city, ate and slept on my schedule. No one knew where I was, what I
was doing, or whom I was doing it with. I was completely, deliriously
anonymous. I took risks that in New York would have triggered panic
attacks. I stayed out late, talked to strangers, and walked the streets
alone. I went places I didn't know with people I'd just met. I ate
anything, and left my windows open at night. For the first time in my
life, I was fearless.

As a relatively attractive young American, I was invited to a lot of
parties and clubs. The hottest club at the time was called Les Bains
Douches. One night I was with some friends, standing outside, waiting on line to get in. The bouncer saw me, parted the crowd, and
let me waltz right in. As I went through the doors, he said, "*Bonsoir,*
Mademoiselle Schiffer."

He thought I was Claudia Schiffer, the German supermodel then at the peak of her fame. This was the ultimate proof of one thing: I was really good with makeup.

I'd go out to a club and meet five people. They'd invite me out the next night, and I'd meet ten more. Soon I was going out to bars, parties, or clubs every night of the week. During the day, I studied French literature and language, and strolled through museums. I fell in love with feminist author Simone de Bouvoir and existentialist Jean-Paul Sartre. I was a regular at the Musée Picasso, the Rodin Museum, and, of course, the Louvre. Mona Lisa and I got close. I spent afternoons staring at Monet's water lilies. My French improved dramatically. I arrived sounding like Inspector Clouseau. Within a couple of months, I was Isabelle Huppert (or so I pretended). I had American friends through school, but we spoke French to each other. It was part of the program.

I was in a new place, dreaming, thinking, reading in a new language, seeing new things. I felt myself change from my head to my toes. Reinvention wasn't only possible here, it was actually happening.

In the land of champagne, Pernod, and Grand Marnier, I didn't touch alcohol. For that matter, I refused the vials of cocaine that were constantly waved under my nose at the clubs. Living in Paris had allayed a lot of my anxieties, but I was still afraid of feeling out of control of my body. Some of my friends thought it was weird that I refused to partake in the drugs and booze that flowed Seine-like in my direction. But no one pressured me to do it. I was high on life. I didn't need the boost.

I met a man named Alexandre at a party. We were seated at the same table and he spoke fluent English. I spoke French, trying to improve, but he wanted to practice his English. We got to talking and didn't stop all night. He looked like Bruce Willis, minus the cocky American swagger. In its place, Alexandre radiated European sophistication. He was dark and masculine and had a twinkle in his eye. There was something nerdy about him, which was actually an asset in his business. He was involved in the management of high-end Paris nightclubs. He was on the business side, having a degree from a top-ranked French business school. Like me, he didn't drink. We discovered this at our first dinner when we both ordered Perrier.

Enter boyfriend number three.

The sweetest part of having a boyfriend in the business: I got in everywhere. He had a free, all-access pass into the world of Paris nightlife. Not just the VIP rooms, but the underground clubs that mere mortals didn't know existed. At his own clubs, he would arrange for agencies to send over models. The models brought in the rock stars. The rock stars attracted actors and wealthy Europeans. Everyone was beautiful. Everyone was chic. And they were all wasted out of their minds. It was like living in a Fellini movie with French dubbing. And Alexandre knew everyone.

One night, I found myself at a banquette with all the supermodels of the era—Naomi, Claudia, Cindy—with bottles of champagne in front of us. They were aloof. Smoking, drinking, and dressed to the nines in a chic yet casual way. They didn't talk to me. I wasn't a model or part of their club (like a flashback to junior high). But I was dazzled by them, and watched them joke with one another and dance with my jaw unhinged. Men flocked to the table. When Naomi and Cindy ignored them, they asked me what agency I modeled for. I guess I was blond enough to pass. When I danced on the tables with the models in my high boots and tights, I blended.

On any given night, I didn't know who would come through the doors of Alexandre's clubs. Celebrity sightings were commonplace. And then a man came into the club du jour, and knocked the ennui right out of me. Sylvester Stallone, my junior high fantasy boyfriend, arrived with his model wife, Jennifer Flavin. Alexandre welcomed him and introduced us. Sly was much shorter than me. I had to lean down for a double-cheek kiss. He smelled like soap and the well-oiled leather of boxing gloves. I was in heaven! Later that night, I was on the dance floor with hundreds of people jumping up and down. Alexandre and Sly were watching me from a balcony.

Allegedly, Sly said, "Yo, Alex. Your girlfriend can really dance."

When I played this back in my head, he sounded like Rocky Balboa ("Yo!"). The next night we all had dinner together. Sly was delightful in real life, a lovely person. I sat next to him, and we shared a dessert. After that teenage dream come true, I was officially addicted to the nightlife. The thought of a quiet evening at home made me antsy. Alexandre was only too happy to have me at his side at the club. I loved being his girlfriend, too. Alexandre was no-nonsense, not a Pepé Le Pew arm-kissing French romantic. His brain was more than enough to seduce me. He knew everyone in Paris and I felt connected and protected.

We fought sometimes. Being a creature of the nightlife was a blast, but it was also fast and furious. A lot could happen when you stayed up until dawn. The intensity was stressful and overwhelming. Every day, I was studying and challenged at my classes. Every night, sex, drugs, and booze surrounded us. Even though we did not partake, the temptation was always there. I flirted with guys. Alexandre didn't love that. Nonetheless, I was head over heels (flats, whatever) with our life together. I couldn't imagine anything going wrong between us.

It was my honeymoon in Paris, with Paris. Like all honeymoons, though, it ended too quickly.

*   *   *

After two semesters abroad, I was supposed to return to Vassar for senior year. If I didn't, I might not graduate with my class. I flew to New York, drove to Poughkeepsie, wheeled and dealed, and came up with a plan to earn enough credits to graduate. I stayed at Vassar for one long semester and got my degree. Finally, I returned to Paris as a student in New York University's Masters French Program. I was back in the place I loved, doing what I loved. My year abroad had changed me inside and out. The result of my reinvention: I felt like a foreigner at home.

I moved in to Alexandre's converted garage loft in the Bastille area. Our apartment was rough around the edges—as was our relationship. The fighting got worse. I hadn't really realized it when I lived in my own apartment, but Alexandre had a bit of a temper.

One day, a New York pal called and said, "My friend Jennifer is coming to Paris. Can you take care of her?" She showed up in jeans and a ponytail, looking exactly like what she was—an Upper East Side Jewish princess, recently graduated from the University of Pennsylvania. She reminded me of New York. For the first time in a year and a half, I felt nostalgic for home. I did not look like a Vassar graduate. I'd gone native, a wild club chick, in miniskirts, sparkly tops, big hair, and dramatic makeup. Jennifer and I became friends instantly and continued to take Paris by storm.

The minute Jennifer entered my life, so did her mother. She called every day to tell me what Jennifer should eat and whom she should date—only wealthy men. I didn't have a controlling Jewish mother. I had a sweet shiksa mom who respected boundaries. Listening to Jennifer's mom call the shots was more of a culture shock than living in Paris.

I started spending a lot of time with Jennifer and other Americans, including Lizzy Guber, the daughter of film producer Peter Guber. We were a fast group, and really lived it up. We studied during the day, and indulged in restaurants and clubs at night. Nothing seedy or dangerous. We were actually pretty staid. We called ourselves the Golden Girls because we acted like old ladies. For lunch, it was the Ritz. For dinner, Stresa or Le Grand Venise, an incredible Italian restaurant, were our favorites. We didn't think twice about eating pasta every night. Carbs weren't the enemy back then.

Fashion was such a huge part of living in Paris. I tried on all kinds of looks. One week, I was decked out head-to-toe in classic Chanel. The next, I was in Jean Paul Gaultier. Jennifer, Lizzie, and I combed through Hermés sample sales. I started collecting Birkin bags before they were popular in America.

No one knew about my leg, except the New Yorkers and Alexandre. He never saw my stump, though. I could tell he was the queasy type. I was careful about that, and kept my prosthesis on at all times. Paris, like New York, was a walking city. The abrasions turned my stump into steak tartare. I needed to find a prosthetist in Paris to make adjustments. Through Alexandre, I met an artist named Yves Corbassiere. He was at least eighty, and wore a big black hat. He hung around the clubs and always had a group of beautiful, sexy young women with him. He wore a prosthetic leg, too, and connected me with an alleged genius prosthetist outside of Paris. Although that turned out to be a disappointment, I was thrilled to have made a friend of Corbassiere.

One day, he asked me to lunch. The restaurant ceiling had a Michelangelo reproduction painted on it. At night, the retractable roof would open up, and you could see the sky while you ate. He knew every precious spot like this in the city, and loved sharing them with his friends. He solicitously poured my water and was adorably fussy about the food. Living was an art form to him. Everything had to be just so. He spoke passionately about any topic. And wherever he went, sexy women surrounded him. At our lunch, they were relegated to a nearby table, and kept looking over at us.

When we left the restaurant, Corbassiere took my arm. The girls followed behind us in a row.

Muses, groupies, hired girlfriends, whatever those women were, they kept his passion burning. An artist needed his inspiration. I would have loved it if Corbassiere painted me, but we never got around to that, regrettably.

My parents came for a visit. Although they liked Alexandre, they gently insinuated that he was not right for me. I was getting tired of nightclubs and the party people that came with that scene. The novelty was wearing off. I stayed home some nights, and Alexandre didn't show up until dawn. I started resenting him. We fought more often, loudly, like a French movie couple. It seemed romantic, for a week. But then I just felt sick of it. I hadn't come to Paris to argue. I'd come for freedom. But the relationship started to feel uncomfortably restrictive. This lifestyle was vapid. Our fights were ridiculous. I told Alexandre how I felt, and it just launched another French-accented screaming match with wild hand gestures.

Jennifer's living situation changed, and she needed a place to stay. I invited her to move into Alexandre's. That might not have been the best idea. His apartment was a wide-open loft. It was eclectic and cool, but there wasn't a lot of privacy. Alexandre and I weren't getting along well. I thought having Jennifer around would put him on his best behavior.

She came home one afternoon when Alexandre and I were in the midst of another row about our lifestyle. I said, "I'm done with it. I can't do it anymore."

Then he put his hands on my shoulders and shoved me so hard I went reeling. At the same moment Jennifer opened the door. I flew across the room, right past her. She stood there in shock at the sight. I landed on the floor, hitting it hard on my hip. Like my accident, there was no pain at first. Only shock. I glanced across the room at Alexandre. His chest was heaving and he looked furious. It was as if Jennifer didn't exist. She actually giggled from fear.

Then she came over to me, scooped me up, and got me out of the loft. In a daze, I went along to a nearby café. She ordered us coffee.

"How long has this been going on?" she asked.

"What?"

"The pushing? Has he hit you?"

"No!" He had pushed me before, though. Would he hit me the next time? I had no idea. "He's just afraid of losing me. It can come out as anger."

She was silent for a minute, and I realized how irrational that sounded.

"It's time you went home," said Jennifer. "You have to get away from this guy. Come back to New York with me."

She was scheduled to return to New York in a week. I'd been in Alexandre's orbit for a long time by then. His night world became mine. I was swept up in it, and had lost perspective on myself. Jennifer was like a protective Jewish mother herself at age twenty-one. She shined a harsh new light on my French affair. I'd accepted Alexandre's possessiveness, his temper, and his criticism as part of who he was. In the artificial atmosphere of the demimonde, I thought that passionate fighting and fierce possessiveness were proof of his love for me. But they were just proof of how far I'd strayed from my own true nature. I'd let a man turn me into something I swore I would never be: someone who felt bad for herself.

Even if Alexandre hadn't shoved me, our relationship wouldn't have lasted. He was thirty-three, a confirmed bachelor. Being part of the club scene perpetuated his youth. He had no intention of growing up. If I stayed with him, our future would be more of the same: clubbing, partying, big fights—possibly escalating from shoving to hitting—and passionate make-up sessions. Children, marriage, and a quiet, safe home life were out of the question. I'd been raised on crazy in New York and had come three thousand miles to replicate the old patterns. If I was going to be unstable, I might as well do it at home. I missed my parents.

I had no regrets about my three years in Paris. I learned to speak fluent French and learned a lot about myself. I had my master's in French literature. I was twenty-three years old, an official adult. It was time to go home, and for my real life to begin.

"You're right," I told Jennifer. "I'm ready to go back."

I flew back to New York within the week.

I couldn't as easily swan back into my old life. Paris had changed me. My old friendships felt forced. It seemed like everyone had moved on to a new life with jobs, college friends, and relationships. But none of that was as disturbing as events at home.

While I was away, my parents had been in turmoil. They kept the truth from me that Dad's business was in serious trouble. They decided to put the Kenilworth apartment on the market and were moving to Miami. Dad was in his sixties. Mom was just fifty. They were too young to make the traditional Jewish migration south.

"We need to make a change," said Dad. "I can't keep up anymore. I'm done with it. I am sick of New York City combat living." If they got a good price for the New York apartment, they could live off the profit for the rest of their lives in Florida. The move wasn't a complicated geographical calculation. It was basic math.

"You can live in the apartment until it's sold," Dad told me. "But then you have to get your own place." They left the city to search for a house in Miami. I stayed alone in my childhood home, soon to belong to someone else. I spent many nights by myself, knocking around that apartment. I'd lived there since I was six. Not all the memories were happy ones. But they were mine.

I'd left New York in part to get away from my parents and my old life. Those five years, between the ages of eighteen and twenty-three, were the only years I spent off the island of Manhattan. I had the college experience. I'd lived a Moulin Rouge fantasy in Paris. Being a flamingo out of water, as it were, had been exciting. But I was ready to start my adult life in my natural habitat, to make a nest and a name for myself.

CHAPTER SIX

Prune

In the grand tradition of overeducated, underemployed women who don't know what to do with their lives, I went to law school. I'd been working at a life insurance company for a couple of years, and talking about death all day long made we want to kill myself. I had a passion for criminal law and a big mouth, so pursuing a law degree seemed like the obvious career choice. I took the LSAT and went to Benjamin N. Cardozo School of Law in the West Village of Manhattan.

Part of me thought of law school as a cop-out. I had my bachelor's degree and a master's in French. Now a law degree? I'd become a perpetual student. But it was better than sitting in the office discussing life expectancy rates all day. The job was really starting to depress me.

In law school, I came back to life—my classes were fascinating. My favorite teacher was Barry Scheck, who taught while he was working as one of OJ's defense attorneys. I'd take a class, and then watch him talk about DNA evidence on TV that night. Now *that* was cool.

At the risk of sounding like a stupid girl, I defined eras of my life by my boyfriend at the time. When I was in law school, I met a man named Jonathan through a mutual friend of a friend. We were introduced at a party and Jonathan called to ask me out.

And so began the early Jonathan Period. I hadn't had a serious boyfriend since Paris. Jonathan was the all-American antidote to Alexandre. He was funny, outgoing, tall, and tan. He wore his hair slicked back, like Leonardo DiCaprio in *The Great Gatsby*. The combo of athletic and intellectual was irresistibly sexy. He was a business student at Columbia University; I was a first-year law student. We were both native Manhattanites. At exactly the right moment, Jonathan reminded me what was incomparable about New York. Any day, around any corner, you could fall in love.

I fell just as hard for his kooky family. His mother, Edith, was a real downtown character. Super thin, she wore tight, short clothing and chunky ethnic jewelry. Her lips were extralarge, even in the bee-stung-lips nineties. Edith had to be in her fifties when I knew her, but she had the dewy soft skin of a newborn baby and her hair was jet black. Picture a skinny, older, stylish version of Veronica from the Archie comics, with huge lips. Edith was eccentric and superstitious. She threw salt over her shoulder, knocked wood, or kissed a mezuzah whenever something about the future was mentioned.

"Don't have sex with my son," she announced one day. "You have to wait until you're married."

At first, I wondered why she thought I hadn't *already* had sex with Jonathan. We'd been together for a while by then. The fact was, despite our serious attraction to each other, Jonathan and I hadn't done "it" yet. I'd been thinking lately that we really should cross that Rubicon. And here she was telling me not to. Was it up to her? I wasn't about to discuss what I had or hadn't done with her son. It was just too weird. Edith might be that cool, but I wasn't.

Dear God, I thought, *was Jonathan telling his mom about our sex life?* (He wasn't.)

"I won't give away the milk," I blurted.

"Good," she said. "I like you, Aviva. I want you and Jonathan to get married. But if you have sex before the wedding, it won't happen. Don't ask me how I know. I just know."

Edith spent a lot of time meditating with crystals and chanting. The incense she burned might've opened up a pathway to the great beyond, and she could see into our future. In her present, she was locked in an absolutely vicious tooth-and-nail divorce battle with Jonathan's father. There was a lot of hatred, bitterness, resentment, and money involved. Edith distrusted men in general. To some extent, that included her own son.

Thus far, in my romantic history, I'd had a great relationship that ended amicably, a good relationship that ended in infidelity, and a tumultuous affair that ended in violence. I was on a downward trend. I believed I could turn that around with Jonathan.

Some of Edith's superstitiousness must have rubbed off on me. I heeded her warning, and held Jonathan off. I wasn't a prude or frigid. I loved sex and had a great time with Jonathan. But we didn't go all the way. Something besides Edith's prediction kept me from going for it. I'd been burned. I'd learned to be wary of throwing myself into an intense relationship that might make me lose sight of my personal goals. Long term, I wanted to be a hotshot attorney, as well as a wife and mother. If not having intercourse made that possible, I'd wait for it. There was also something worthwhile about maintaining a little mystery in the relationship.

After a year of dating, Jonathan proposed. We were in the Hamptons at his dad's house. We went for dinner in Sag Harbor at a restaurant in the American Hotel. At the end of the meal, Jonathan got on one knee in front of the whole restaurant and asked me to marry him. He presented a four-karat emerald-cut diamond with very elegant side stones. Of course, I said yes, and the restaurant applauded and cheered.

Edith was thrilled at the news. We told her in person. "Congratulations!" she said, hugging us. Jonathan left the room to make a phone call. She cocked an eyebrow at me. "Don't forget. No cheating on the *rule*. Not before the wedding night."

We hadn't. Not even after that fairy-tale engagement dinner. We might've, but very soon after, sex had to be back burnered. I got an especially nasty abrasion on my stump. It was about two square inches of red, pulpy raw flesh. I was used to that, but this time, it just wouldn't heal. It was puffy and really sensitive.

Jonathan urged me to see a plastic surgeon. I was long past due for a new, thicker skin graft. I made an appointment with yet another doctor. He took one look at my abrasion and visibly paled. "This is terribly infected," he said. "You have to check into the hospital tonight."

Not *again*.

The dreaded osteomyelitis, that potentially fatal bone infection, had finally come. It'd been looming like the sword of Damocles over my head (leg) for nineteen years. That was long enough, said Destiny. I checked into Beth Israel North Hospital right away, continuing on my tour of every Manhattan hospital on the grid, for a series of MRIs and other tests to confirm the diagnosis.

They put me on IV antibiotics. The drugs snatched me back

from the brink. I survived my third (fourth?) close call. You know, all those near-death experiences, and I had yet to see a white light or my beloved dogs Clever and Sandy panting at the entrance of heaven, beckoning me in. I was starting to feel a little resentful.

While I recovered in the hospital, I had a consult with a renowned hand surgeon. He said, "I'm going to give you a gift on a silver platter. If you amputate your leg below the knee, you'll have a totally new, better life."

I'd heard that before. Various experts over the years had suggested I get a BKA, a.k.a. a below-the-knee amputation. It would mean no more abrasions or pain, a slimmer prosthesis, and better mobility. I hadn't opted for that surgery, though. It seemed insane. Why on earth would anyone elect to have her leg sawed off? I had horrific memories of my past surgeries. Missing a foot, I figured, was sexier than missing half a leg. I cared a lot about being sexy. Always had, always will. So much so that if a doctor had said years ago, "If you get rid of your leg below the knee, you'll be way sexier," I probably would have done it sooner.

Something about this hand surgeon broke through the wall I'd built against voluntary surgery. If it would really get rid of pain and those hateful abrasions, maybe it wasn't such a crazy idea.

"Would you do it?" I asked my friend Sarah. I knew she'd be completely honest with me. Historically, she had zero filter.

"You would lose five pounds overnight," she said. "Seriously, for quality of life, you should go for it. I'd do it in a second."

"I'm getting married in six months," I said.

"Which is why you should do it now."

Sarah had no ulterior motive. She wasn't a doctor looking for a job. She was only thinking of what was best for me. More than anyone, she knew how much I wanted to start my life with Jonathan with my best foot—well, my only foot—forward. My worst fear was that the abrasions would prevent me from being a capable mother. I did *not* want to be a slave to my wounds when I had children to look after. I imagined myself failing to catch a child who dashed into traffic or ran ahead at the park. The abrasions had slowed me down for decades. I had to do whatever I could to be quick and strong before I committed to being Jonathan's wife, and the mother of his children. I mustered my courage and scheduled the surgery.

During the four weeks between scheduling and having the procedure, my reservations faded completely. When I was six, and I had that first amputation, I remembered thinking, "If it stops the pain, *great.*" This new surgery brought up the same anticipation. I'd been in denial about the abrasions for so long. I'd refused to acknowledge the pain. Once I could imagine a life without it, it couldn't come fast enough.

The surgery didn't scare me. Anesthesia, however, was petrifying. As a child, being put under made me violently ill and disoriented. I'd developed a phobia about it, believing that if I were put to sleep (like Clever and Sandy), I would never wake up. *I'll be the one healthy twenty-six-year-old who dies on the table,* I thought. The select few who knew about my panic attacks and hypochondria back then (pre–*Real Housewives*) called me "a blonde Woody Allen." Actually, I made Woody Allen look chill. Here's a running list of (some of) the things that freak me out:

Small planes
Heights
Driving on highways
Going over bridges
Anesthesia

Terrorists

Rapists coming in through the bedroom window

Factory-farmed meat

Aluminum foil

Teflon

Drugs! Recreational, prescription, over the counter, pain killers. You name it, I'm afraid of it.

Pesticides

Inflammation, which can cause cancer; which reminds me . . .

Cancer

ALS

Crossing against the light

Leaving a hat on the bed (this shit is deadly)

Some spiders (big ones are fine; it's the little things that get me)

The dark

Prison

Being trapped on an elevator with Ramona Singer (oh, I kid, Ramona . . .)

Okay, several of those aren't real sources of anxiety for me. But they could be. The point is, I don't choose my anxieties. They choose me. If I could will them away, of course I would! But my neurological and psychological makeup can't be changed. Medications would only work to a point, but it's weirdly arbitrary how some things freak me out, and others don't at all. The only way to handle it is to avoid panic attack triggers and be prepared with soothing strategies (like an iPod full of calming music). And laughing. I always joke about it, even mid-meltdown. Making light of a panic attack doesn't cancel it out. But it does give me something to do in the meantime. One trick I've learned as a professional worrier is that you can't feel fear and love simultaneously. Just kissing Reid and/or the kids really helps.

In our presurgery consult, Dr. Elton Strauss, the orthopedic surgeon, and I talked about the procedure. He'd do the wet work, and then Dr. Chun, a plastic surgeon, would step in to make a special flap so I'd have extrathick skin on the bottom of the residual leg. I would never have another abrasion. It sounded *wonderful*. The surgery would take place back where I started, at Mount Sinai Hospital.

I asked Dr. Strauss, "Can I stay awake for the surgery with an epidural?" I didn't want to be knocked out, just numb below the waist.

"You want to be awake for your amputation?" he asked. "Never heard that one before."

I explained my fears, and he agreed to do the surgery with an epidural—an injection of anesthetic directly into my spinal cord, the same thing women get for C-sections. That was a relief. I skipped home from that appointment, actually looking forward to getting rid of the chronically infected leg that served no purpose except filling a bulky, ugly prosthesis.

I'd been researching a sleek upgrade. Prosthetics had made leaps and bounds since the seventies. I could get one with carved foam to match the shape of my right leg. I'd finally have a decent cushion that created more bounce and flexibility. My upgrade wouldn't be cheap, but I still had plenty of insurance money. What better way to spend it?

Surgery Number Five: Elective Below-the-Knee Amputation of Left Leg

My presurgery bluster fizzled on the day of the operation. I was terrified about the whole anesthesia issue. As I was wheeled into the room, I badgered the anesthesiologist, a woman named Mary, with a million questions. She sized me up as an anxious basket case.

"Get the Valium!" she called out to a nurse.

This time, I took it. Mary gave me *plenty*. The Valium calmed me, but honestly, I didn't like it. I flashed back to being drugged as a child, and feeling weightless and confused. Altered states of consciousness were not fun for me. I appreciated that everyone I knew enjoyed having a few cocktails or some pot. No judgment, but I couldn't stand not feeling like myself.

I lay on the table in the operating room, coming in and out of a drug-induced sleep. Mary sat me up and helped me lean forward to expose my vertebrae. She gave me the epidural, puncturing my spinal cord with a needle and injecting the numbing agent. I started to feel warm from the waist down. She helped me lay back down.

Dr. Strauss appeared. "Okay, Aviva," he said. "We're going to cut off your leg now."

"Go for it," I mumbled.

I could hear everything. The whir of the saw, some crunching and squishing. I could smell cauterized flesh, bone dust, and hot metal. It was Surgery 101. Surgeons had been lopping off limbs with a sharp rock for thousands of years in tents on battlefields. In a modern hospital operating room, it took all of ten minutes. Dr. Chun stepped up to the table to start working on the flap. I felt nothing.

"Can I call my mom?" I asked right there, while I was on the table. I was a big phone person at the time, always connected.

Dr. Strauss said, "Go ahead."

I dialed her number from the OR phone. "Hi, Mom," I slurred.

"Aviva? I thought it was the doctor saying you died."

And I was the paranoid one? "Nope. Not dead. I'm calling to tell you everything is all right. I'm still on the table. Dr. Strauss just powered down the saw."

"Oh, good. I was worried," she said in a small voice. She knew I was in the OR and she was really panicked to get a phone call during the operation. Understandably!

And I was worried about her being worried. This was a pervasive theme in our relationship, my anxiety about her anxiety—that it might lead her to drink. I said, "I'm going to hang up. See you in recovery soon."

"That's another first," said Dr. Strauss. "Amputation without general anesthesia. And making a call during an operation."

He seemed flabbergasted. I'd given him something to talk about in the hospital cafeteria later.

After surgery, I was wheeled into the recovery room. My fiancé and mother had to wait in another room. The Valium faded, but I was still paralyzed from the waist down, and completely alone. I couldn't sit up to see my leg, so I didn't know how it looked. I started to panic. And so another phobia was born: the fear of being alone in the recovery room. Finally, I was wheeled into a regular room and told that my family would be joining me soon. I looked down at the stump. It was so short. So abbreviated. I hadn't thought I'd miss the leg that had given me so much trouble. But now that it was gone, I felt depressed. For the first time ever, I cried about my loss of limb. It was so unlike me.

And then the epidural wore off.

Now I really had something to cry about. The pain was indescribable. I writhed on the bed. Nurses offered to give me a morphine injection. I'd had morphine as a child, and it made me feel like I was losing my mind. I would float out of my body—a sensation similar to my panic attacks. I couldn't stand that. I couldn't stand the pain. I'd been smug about not being afraid of the amputation, and looking forward to ending the pain of abrasions. But I hadn't thought about the postop pain. I had no idea it would be this bad. I was overwhelmed, and couldn't think of anything else. Jonathan and Mom couldn't do much to comfort me, but they stayed in the room while I rode it out.

When Dr. Strauss checked in on me, I complained about pain. He said, "So take the drugs."

"I can't," I said.

A postop patient who refused morphine. Another first. "Either take the drugs or deal with the pain," he said. Gee, thanks, Doc! I don't know how it hadn't occurred to me that those would be my only options, but now that I was in this predicament I searched desperately for alternatives.

"Can I get another epidural to get me through the next few days?" For one reason or another, as he explained, that wasn't advisable.

"How about hitting me on the head until I black out?"

He laughed. I wasn't joking. I kept asking for alternatives. The doctor was sick of me by that point. And I don't blame him; I was a major pain in the ass.

Jonathan slept in the hospital room. My dad visited. A friend from college, Paul, now a very well known dermatologist, swung by. I'd always leaned on him with my hypochondria. He was in medical school then, and very cool about hospitals and surgery. In my room, he put his feet up on my bed and chatted like we were chilling at home. I loved him for that.

Mom was jumpy and irritable. When I was little, she was 1,000 percent present and focused. This time around, she was distant and grouchy. She sat and read the paper testily, crinkling the pages with each turn. When I talked to friends and Jonathan, Mom acted annoyed and made rude comments or sighed heavily. It was obvious she would have rather been anywhere else. Being in the hospital with me again must have dredged up some terrible memories for her. Also, at the same time, her brother was dying with pancreatic cancer.

In addition to all that, Mom was itching for a drink.

I was so absorbed in my pain, I didn't sort that out. All I knew was that my angelic mom was lacking compassion. She was not her warm loving self. I'd probably exhausted my lifetime allowance of maternal patience, comfort, and support years ago. Mom had taken me to hundreds of doctors' appointments, and spent weeks beside my hospital bed already. I was no longer a helpless child. But at six or twenty-six, when you're in pain and in the hospital, you just want your mother. As a mother myself, I can't imagine not wanting to be there—physically and emotionally—for my children no matter how old they are. Then again, I couldn't imagine what it is like to be in the grips of alcoholism.

My fiancé, on the other hand, was a champ. He slept in the room with me and asked, "What can I do for you, Fever?" (My nickname. Jonathan used to say he had "Aviva fever." Edith and his sister made it stick.) He proved at an early stage in the game that he loved me through thick and thin. This was decidedly a thick week. The whole gig was not pretty. After five days, I was released. I only took Advil and my wound healed beautifully.

I still had to be fit for a new leg. In the meantime, I wore a postop prosthesis and used crutches. Jonathan and I flew to Los Angeles for a wedding during that waiting period. He helped me in and out of taxis, and always walked slowly at my side. He didn't rush me or lose patience. In our hotel room, he hung up his shirts, and kept the bathroom clean. He looked sensational in his tux.

I thought, *What am I waiting for?* The man had just gotten me through major, highly unsexy surgery. How could I go through that experience with him but not have intercourse? Edith's waiting for the wedding night "rule" was ridiculous. I was under her spell—a goodwitch spell, but still.

That weekend, we did it.

Afterward, basking in the glow, I heard Edith's warning in my head. We were in love, engaged, the sex was good. What could be the harm in doing it before the wedding night? I laughed to myself. *How did I let her warning get to me?* I wondered.

"What's so funny?" he asked.

"Nothing."

The wedding would be at the Round Hill Club in Jamaica. Our three hundred guests had made their hotel reservations and booked their flights. Edith and my mother helped me plan the wedding. Mom's mood rallied as the date drew nearer, despite her feeling anxious about the whole wedding. Decorating and taking care of her family were strengths. Big parties and traditions were not her thing. My father and mother were against big weddings altogether, finding them to be forced and tacky. Nonetheless, they were paying for mine, and went along with my dreams of a big, beautiful destination wedding.

Jonathan's father, on the other hand, was not a fan of the plan. He thought a wedding in Jamaica was ridiculous. (He was probably right.) More than that, he was against the wedding, period, regardless of the location. A bit of a playboy himself, he thought his son was way too young to settle down. Jonathan respectfully disagreed. They argued about it. His dad kept needling him and pressuring him to reconsider. One weekend when I was not around but Jonathan was, his father brought some hot young women home. For what purpose? It was really bizarre. The tension between father and son affected our relationship, too. I talked with Jonathan about his father, and found myself in the unnerving position of defending the man who was trying to break up my engagement.

A brilliant real estate guy, Jonathan's dad was gifted at negotiating. When words failed him, he broke out the heavy artillery. One month before the wedding, he delivered a prenup to my family's lawyers. It said basically that if Jonathan and I ever divorced, regardless of how long our marriage lasted or how many children we had, I wouldn't be entitled to a dime.

Was he trying to run me off?

It made no sense to me. I had my own money. My parents had resources. I was in school to become a lawyer and would be more than capable of generating my own income. I never had a money mind the way some people do. I hadn't really thought about the financial side of marriage, at least not until Jonathan's father brought it front and center. Money was his wedge. He drove it between us with all his might.

My lawyer begged me not to sign the prenup. She told me it was unfair and the most extreme prenup she had ever seen. "It's a ridiculous document. Do you really want to marry a man whose father is trying to screw you over?"

I signed it. I didn't care about Jonathan's money.

Even then, his dad kept calling Jonathan and encouraging him not to marry me. Why? Edith's theory was that he didn't want Jonathan to make the mistake of marrying at all. (Like I said, their divorce was vicious.) She also suspected that the father hoped that his son would be his single-guy buddy. I was standing on crutches in the way.

Jonathan felt the pressure. We started fighting constantly. Anything I said came off as confrontational. He was in a foul mood, and fought any effort I made to turn it around. His temper came out. I hadn't seen it before in nearly two years of dating. But I started to flash to Paris, with Alexandre.

That scared me. I peeled back a corner of the perfect picture I'd painted of our life together, and found a blank canvas underneath.

Just like with Alexandre, I started asking myself, *What do Jonathan and I really share? What do we have in common?* I was attracted to his outdoorsy lifestyle, but I didn't participate in it. He'd been frustrated by my lack of interest in biking and hiking for a while, just as he didn't see why he had to go to the Philharmonic and the Met with me. It wasn't only our divergent hobbies and interests that started to bother me. I was seeing him in a new light. His newly revealed temper reminded me of the way his father talked to me and treated Edith. Jonathan had been loving and patient in the hospital. What changed? Now he snapped and seemed perpetually annoyed. I was the same person. But something changed between us. We'd been happy. And then, in the span of a month, we were miserable.

Edith's warning rose again in my mind. I realized with a jolt that things went downhill soon after we had sex.

I'd given away the milk. And our relationship soured.

We had yet another big fight. He hung up on me. It was the day after his bachelor party, and one week before the wedding. I went to his mom's house where he was living and gave him back his ring. I couldn't risk marrying a man with a bad temper. A rumor went around that I canceled the wedding due to a lewd bachelor party. Ridiculous.

A lot of New York society had been invited to the wedding. They'd bought plane tickets and were now stuck with them. Both of our families suffered fallout. Dad called each guest personally and apologized. His secretary returned all the gifts. Some of our guests went to Jamaica anyway, but a lot canceled. A young designer and friend named Tory Burch (yes, the very same) who worked at Vera Wang made my custom gown and bridesmaid dresses at no cost. The dresses were outstanding. Each bridesmaid dress was going to be a bright, solid color spaghetti-strap tank with a giant tulle skirt in the same bright color. So one bridesmaid was going to have bright yellow, another fuchsia, and so on. These dresses had been featured in *Vogue* that year and were divine. I always wondered if Tory was annoyed that they wouldn't be seen by our guests or photographed for the *New York Times* wedding section. She was too elegant to ever show anything to me but kindness. To date, Tory has never brought it up.

Jonathan took comfort in pleasing his father. His mother was upset. My parents were relieved. They weren't upset about the lost cost of the wedding. They wanted what was best for me. Jonathan's father was, of course, vindicated. I proved him right about nearly every terrible thing he'd said about me, marriage, and women in general. Although my concerns about Jonathan's temper were real, they did not turn out to be accurate—not by a long shot. He and his wife of many years are blissfully happy and have two beautiful children whom they adore. He and I are still friends.

I'd ended the relationship, but I was heartbroken. Another open, raw wound. I handled the pain by making it worse. A week after the breakup, the same day I would have been getting married, I hooked up with another man. Remember Paul, the college friend turned dermatologist? Him.

I finally fulfilled my lifelong doctor fetish, but at a cost. The only thing I could say in my own defense was that I was flailing. Although I had long been terrified of drugs taking away my control, my erratic behavior was the larger threat. I just needed . . . *something* . . . so desperately. Jonathan wasn't the rock I sought. And then Paul, an old trusted friend, was there. We became an item *because* I'd been crying on his shoulder about the breakup. One thing led to another. Our relationship only lasted a couple of months. He ended it.

I was having lunch with friends at Fred's restaurant in the basement at Barneys weeping and weeping about Paul. But really, it was everything: Jonathan, my own behavior, guilt, shame, embarrassment, residual pain about the surgery, and that horrible feeling that I didn't know what I was doing or why I was behaving like this.

"Losing Paul is like losing my right arm," I cried.

"What did he say when he broke up with you?" asked my friend Kelly.

"He didn't want to be the rebound guy," I said. "Which makes no sense. He doesn't even play basketball!"

Blonde moment number 4,328. I didn't know what a rebound relationship was. It was like the time in fourth grade when a boy asked me if I knew what a blow job was and I said, "Oh, yeah, I always get a blow job after a haircut."

I could claim "young and stupid" only to a point. I'd hurt others, and myself, in what I came to think of as the Pruning Year. I didn't always think things through, or imagine beyond the moment when I brought out the sheers to cut back. I certainly hadn't counted on the pain I experienced and caused. Having elective surgery and calling off the wedding were both drastic amputations, and the right decisions to make. At my low moments in the aftermath, I hoped that the pruning of broken parts and relationship would clear the way for new things to grow.

CHAPTER SEVEN

Switch

My father was born Jewish. My mother was born Lutheran. Neither was observant. We always decorated a Christmas tree growing up, but it wasn't Christian or Jewish. We never went to church or temple. I didn't have a bat mitzvah at thirteen. The extent of my religious upbringing was to say, "Oh, my God!" when we got good news, and to say, "Holy shit!" when we got bad news. We took a sort of spiritual journey (to hell) that month in India with Sai Baba. His cult was nondenominational. He welcomed gullible people of all faiths.

Religion hadn't played an important part—any part, really—in my life. So it might seem strange that in the aftermath of the Jonathan/Paul debacle, I became obsessed with a rebbitzin—the wife of a rabbi—and started going to Torah classes a couple of times a week.

I was a bit lost, and wide open to direction. Jennifer's mom, Cheryl, had taken the Torah class and loved it. I joined her one evening at the Jewish Center on Seventy-fourth Street and West End Avenue. The rebbitzin looked like Tammy Faye Baker, but prettier. She had the fake eyelashes and a short blond wig. (FYI: Many religious Jewish married women wear wigs.) She was tiny and well dressed with perfectly wrapped, long manicured nails. At the lesson, a nice group of secular Jews would sit around and hang on the rebbitzin's every word.

It was way better than Sai Baba.

The rebbitzin—Reb—explained the Jewish Bible and laws in a way that made total sense to me. Something clicked. I found myself nodding along, liking what I heard. Religion could be a part of my life. It should be. Being connected to traditions, history, and something larger than myself would fill a hole inside that I didn't know existed, until I felt it being filled up. I started going to classes twice a week, three times.

Although I was very single, I'd been thinking a lot about my future kids. Coming from a mixed, nutty household, I wanted to prove the opposite to my children. My husband and I would share values and common faith, and give them a steady, unified family life. A half-and-half agnostic, I would have to pick a side of the fence to come down on. All of my friends were Jewish. I lived in New York. If I were leaning toward Judaism, Reb's classes sealed the deal.

I learned the history, traditions, and observations. Some of the practices fit my lifestyle, like keeping my legs covered. Some didn't. According to Jewish law, a woman is not allowed to have sex during her period. I kind of got that one, as sexist as it sounded (menstruating women being unclean, etc.). A five-day break once a month could create a little mystery and build anticipation, two things missing in long-term relationships. The practice wasn't necessarily for me, but I could see how it could work. Same thing with keeping kosher. It was really like any restrictive diet. When you sat down at a restaurant, you could look at a menu and know right away what you could and couldn't eat. In the right light, it was just a good way to simplify your life.

The Torah classes brought in all kinds of people of different ages, races, and genders. I met a man there, an Iranian Jew named Ricky. (Yes, there are Jews in Iran, and China, and Africa. The diaspora covered the globe. You could find at least one Jew just about anywhere—even Texas.) How many gentile girls went to Torah classes and wound up falling in love with a Persian man? What were the odds? About the same as getting your foot stuck in a barn cleaner.

The opposite of a bookish pale New York Jewish neb type, Ricky was tall, dark, virile, and muscular. I wasn't a Rob Lowe or Michael J. Fox kind of girl. I liked men big and strong—and hairy. Ricky was all that. He was older than me, and seemed to have his life together. He came from a successful real estate family (I know, I know; another one), and worked in the business. His exotic looks were a plus, but he could have been as white bread as I was. We had intense chemistry. We would have found each other from opposite ends of Yankee Stadium.

We started having coffee after class. Coffee. Not a drink. He was straitlaced. He told me more about his family. His parents were born in Iran and moved to the North Shore of Long Island with many members of their extended family. Ricky was born in America, but he was rooted in his family's ancient Persian culture. He lived a double life, in a way: Persian with his family in Great Neck, and a New Yorker in the city.

As attracted as we were, we couldn't have a future unless I became an official Jew. Despite being 50 percent Jewish, according to their law, I was 100 percent gentile. Mom wasn't a member of the tribe.

That meant I wasn't either. (Why does Jewishness come down only on the maternal line? When these laws were written thousands of years ago, paternity couldn't be proven. If you were born of a Jewish mother, however, you were sure to have her genes.) Ricky's family was very religious. Marrying an American was even a stretch. A non-Jew? Forget it.

I didn't convert for Ricky, but he was an important part in the decision. The process wasn't going to be easy. I couldn't just say, "Shalom! I'm a Jew! Let's nosh." For me to become a Jew, I had to study the Torah and go through a process that included a ritual "mikvah" submersion. It's sort of like a baptism for adults—but naked, with bagels and lox after. If you've heard of a mikvah, it's probably in the context of a bath women take after they finish their periods. It represented a cleansing before the husband and wife can have sex again. The same tub was used for conversions as well. (Don't worry—there is a lot of chlorine in the water. Oh, I forgot to put that on my list! I am afraid of chlorine, too. It's a known carcinogen that we soak in when swimming.)

On the big day, I arrived at the mikvah house and went into a little locker room to put on a plain white cotton robe. Next, I moved into another room, like an office, to be interviewed by three rabbis. We sat in chairs and they asked me a series of questions, such as, "Are you a natural blonde?" and "Is that your real leg?" No, really, the questions were about Jewish law and traditions. (FYI: It went deeper than what I learned watching *The Ten Commandments* with Charlton Heston every Passover on TV.) They challenged me on how serious I was about conversion. Satisfied that I'd done my homework and meant business, the rabbis gave their approval for the next step: submersion into the bath.

Two female members of the congregation brought me into the mikvah room. It looked like a spa with a Jacuzzi. The bath water wasn't hot or bubbling. It was just plain warm water, blessed and clean. I took off my robe, and my leg. If you weren't born with it, it doesn't go into the bath. You have to be naked of clothes, jewelry, prostheses, and scrubbed clean of makeup and lotions.

The attendants helped me hop up a couple of steps and sink into the bath. I dunked three times, and was given two blessings by the rabbi outside of the room. They spoke loud enough for me to hear him. And that was it. Done. I'd been symbolically reborn. I went into the mikvah a shiksa, and came out a Jew, possibly the tallest and blondest in New York City.

Every Friday night for Shabbat dinner, Ricky went to Great Neck for a multicourse Persian dinner cooked by his doting mother and sisters. The Persian women would spend the entire day making exotic spicy dishes. I heard stories about this epic meal for months before he finally invited me along. The food alone opened the door to Ricky's culture. I have never had better food in my life—even better than Paris. Rice dishes with raisins and spices, chicken with turmeric, lamb with curry. All of it smelled fantastic, too.

The welcome in Great Neck? A bit chilly. It was a really big deal for Ricky to invite any girlfriend to Friday dinner. And then he showed up with a blond American? I was their worst nightmare. Generally, Iranian Jews did not let their kids marry Americans. When they got a look at me, his family's eyes bugged out like an alien had just walked in. His parents recovered fairly quickly, though, and treated me nicely. They were too sophisticated and polite not to. The house itself was classically suburban and understated. It was large, with a pool. There were Persian books and art and sculptures everywhere and pistachios on the coffee table.

His mom and sisters played by unspoken rules of conduct about cooking and serving. I picked up on one rule right away. Women had to help in the kitchen from the moment you entered the house until dinner was cleaned up, dishes put away. If I finished one task, I had to immediately ask for another.

His mother would say, "No, nononono. You sit."

I said, "But I really want to help."

"If you insist. Go peel those ten pounds of potatoes."

We did this twenty times a night. If I didn't push for more work, Ricky's mom would have forbidden me to come over ever again. They really had this polite fake dance down to a science. It went against my innate no-nonsense character, but I loved Ricky. And I had to win the women in his family over, so I did the dance.

Ricky's father was the patriarch, the king of the house. To do well in New York real estate, you had to be aggressive and tough—and he was very intimidating. He ruled his big family with a quiet, tight grip. According to their way of life, the men worked and the women cooked. A woman who didn't cook wasn't worth her salt, as it were. Even though Ricky knew that I was in law school and respected my independence, he agreed with his dad about the cooking. I was clueless with a skillet. It became an issue.

"I want you to learn to cook like my mother," he said one day. I was taken aback. His culture might insist that women spend their lives in the kitchen. But I knew another tradition. On the Upper West Side, the only thing Jewish women made for dinner was a reservation. But I was desperately, passionately in love with him, and since it mattered to him, I made the effort. So, on the nights I wasn't studying law or Torah, I took cooking classes at Peter Kump's New York cooking school. I made authentic Iranian dinners at my place—I was still at the Kenilworth; the apartment took a while to sell—and brought the food in containers over to Ricky's on Seventy-fourth Street and Second Avenue. I actually got pretty good behind the stove.

If I hadn't been überattracted to him, I would have resented him about the cooking. But I wanted to please him, marry him, and start a family with him. His family had other ideas.

"My father and I had a talk yesterday," said Ricky over one of those dinners I shopped for, cooked, and catered for him. "He was concerned about what would happen if you ended up in a wheelchair. If we got married and had children, what kind of mother could you be in a wheelchair?"

I'd devoted my life since age six to being a 100 percent functional amputee. I'd been able to do everything anyone else could (well, I wasn't a triathlete like Ricky; I did love cheering him on during his races, though). I thought he admired my determination and abilities. To hear his—and his father's—doubts was a real blow.

I couldn't reply for a few seconds. Then I said, "What if you had a heart attack or got hit by a bus and ended up in a wheelchair? Anyone could. I don't get why you're saying this about me."

"That's ridiculous," he said dismissively.

They'd been talking behind my back, and had decided I was feeble and damaged. I wouldn't, in their eyes, have the physical capacity to care for Ricky's children the way a whole and hearty woman would. Ricky's father saw me as a bad bet. Their culling system reminded me of horse traders, inspecting limbs. Any sign of weakness, they moved on to the next animal.

For me, marriage wasn't about passing a physical examination, but about joining souls. A husband and wife should be together in sickness and in health, for richer or for poorer. I would be there for Ricky if he were in a wheelchair, or if his face burned off. Apparently, he didn't feel the same way about me. I think they might've accepted me for being American, fair-colored, and a half-blood Jew, but my leg was an insurmountable issue.

It was a real eye-opener, that conversation. I wondered if my leg had been Jonathan's father's problem with me, too. Jonathan never cared about it. For that matter, Jonathan never expected me to be his cook, maid, and brood mare. Where was Ricky's pushback? He didn't defend me to his father. That had to mean he shared his father's archaic views of marriage, and my unsuitability to tend to him, his house, and his offspring.

I should have said, "Fuck you," and walked out of his house that night.

But I didn't. I was twenty-seven and afflicted by crazy love. I couldn't leave. In fact, I did just the opposite and clung to Ricky and tried to calm his fears. I swore I was as strong as any other woman, and would prove it to him. I threw myself into cooking, and tried more complicated dishes with expensive ingredients.

"Why are you wasting money on these ingredients? My father thinks you spend too much money on clothes, too," he said.

I could not win! He wanted me to cook, and then knocked me for doing the best job I could. He wanted me to look good, but commented on overspending on dresses. He seemed to find fault with everything about me—especially my mother's history with drinking.

My parents were ensconced in Williams Island in Florida, and keen to sell the Kenilworth apartment. I wasn't as eager as they were since I was still living there. The real estate agent was our friend and neighbor Linda Stein, a funny, talky New Yorker through and through. Before she became a broker, she was the manager of the Ramones and a downtown fixture in the '80s rock scene when Blondie, Patti Smith, the Talking Heads, and the Ramones played gigs at the legendary club CBGB. Years later, Linda was tragically murdered by her assistant. Her body was found in her apartment on Fifth Avenue. This past year, one of her daughters died at forty years old of brain cancer. I just don't understand the senseless tragedies that befall us. When I see others experience such irreversible pain and suffering, I become ill with emotional pain.

Linda used her key, and would walk potential buyers through the apartment day and night. David Copperfield and Claudia Schiffer and Rod Stewart came through. It was surreal to be sitting on the couch in my pajamas, look up, and see Linda with a famous actor or singer. I prayed they wouldn't buy the apartment and throw me out on the curb.

My parents needed the money from the sale. My father was a bit neurotic about getting that done, and called from Florida a lot to check on Linda's progress. Mom's anxieties flared up in Florida, too. She didn't do well with the change of scenery. She loved old-world architecture and elegance. Miami was colorful and brash and new. It wasn't to her taste at all. She missed her friends, her haunts, her block. She missed her children. Plus, she was getting older. She'd always taken such care and pride in her beauty. To move to a young city like Miami where every girl in the street had giant fake boobs and a savage tan and flaunted herself in a bikini only underscored Mom's middle age.

She took a hard turn for the worse with her alcoholism. I saw the incremental changes in her. When I flew down to Florida or they came up to the city, I was constantly searching for her stashes. I found bottles of wine under her mattress, in the closets, under towels. It used to be that her personality would change only when she was drunk. But she seemed mentally off all the time now. Was she drunk around the clock? How could anyone be sure? She drank in secret.

I had a bad feeling that something was fundamentally off about her. She was zoned out. It was like she didn't know where she was half the time. Mom was occasionally violent, too, throwing things and punches.

"I'm scared," I told Dad. "Something is wrong with her."

He couldn't see it. But he was with her all the time. The change for him was gradual. I'd see her every two months, and registered a dramatic difference.

Upset and worried about her, I turned to Ricky for an ear and a hug. It was like he put up his palm and said, "Talk to the hand." He did not want to hear about it. I was afraid that alcoholism was also a sign of weakness in his book. Having an alcoholic mother just made me even more unsuitable. So Ricky was no help, and Dad was in deep denial about the severity of the problem.

During one of their visits to New York, I thought my mom was out of control. She stumbled around, her speech slurred. She stared at me like she didn't know me. I found her in the kitchen drinking, and took away her glass. Before, she'd deny the problem or tell me off. But this time, she didn't acknowledge me at all. Silently, zombielike, she just reached for another glass. It was eerie.

I called my doctor and described the symptoms.

"She needs to detox," he said. "Bring her to Lenox Hill tonight."

Dad was against it. He still loathed hospitals and doctors. But I begged him to do it, so we put Mom in the VIP wing at Lenox Hill for detox. I slept at the hospital every night. They gave her drugs that made her hallucinate. She kept trying to leave the hospital, but she did not know what city she was in. Miami? New York? I wasn't sure she knew she was in a hospital. One thing we were sure about: she didn't want to be there. She persistently tried to escape, and had to be tied to the bed. She became violent. Having to see that was traumatizing. It was a turning point. We had to deal with this. No more denial.

They did a CT scan on her brain. It showed that she'd had a series of ministrokes. Possibly, her drinking masked the effects. Probably, her alcoholism caused them. There was nothing we could do about them now. She went on a drug regimen to prevent future brain attacks. I was absolutely despondent. My mother had been having strokes, and no one knew. How on earth had that happened?

The doctors gave us another diagnosis. Mom had irreversible brain shrinkage. The condition was called "wet brain," or Wernicke-Korsakoff syndrome. It was caused by a severe deficiency of thiamine due to alcoholism and alcohol-related poor nutrition. The vitamin deficiencies wrecked her metabolism and that, in turn, caused atrophy of the brain.

"We usually see it in homeless people without access to health care," said the doctor. Her symptoms—confusion, difficulty speaking and focusing, forgetfulness, among other things—fit the diagnosis. All this time, we thought she was just wasted.

"If she'd had thiamine injections a while ago, we might've been able to reverse it," said the doctor. "But with the strokes and progression, vitamin treatments won't do much good."

"She won't get better?" I asked.

"No. But she will get worse if she keeps drinking."

I had no idea how to help her, besides locking her up.

My father was getting tired of all this. He still thought of her alcoholism as a self-inflicted problem that just wouldn't go away. He was anti–mainstream medicine. He looked at Mom full of drugs, tied to the bed, and blamed the doctors for making her worse. He was also low on cash. After two weeks, the bill was over fifty thousand dollars and he was livid about that. He insisted we get her out of the hospital and off the detox drugs. "She's my wife," he said. I acquiesced. They went back to Florida.

I was scared. My mother was increasingly out of reach mentally. This disease was bigger than our ability to help. I didn't feel I could talk to Ricky about it. I chalked up his lack of support as the one flaw in our otherwise perfect relationship. To make up for it, I doubled down on cooking, cleaning, and cheering him on. I felt grateful that he loved me.

What an idiot. I should have told him to fuck off.

Dad checked in with me often. Acceptance that she was really sick sank in. "Your mom," he said one day, "her mind is just . . . going. She doesn't know where she is. She puts things in the wrong place. She forgets things. But she doesn't know she's being forgetful." The symptoms were like those of an Alzheimer's patient.

Dad and I begged her to stop drinking or to agree to go to long-term rehab, like Phoenix House in Arizona. Mom refused to do either. "I'm old enough to make my own decisions. You can't make me."

"Your brain is deteriorating," I said.

"I don't care," she said.

To Dad, I said, "She doesn't understand what she's doing to herself." How could she? She was mentally diminished. She'd had multiple strokes. Her brain was shrinking.

Dad wasn't the most effective policeman. Despite her zoning out, she was still driving. She had use of her credit cards. She came and went as she pleased. He searched for her wine stash and would get rid of it, but she'd just replace it the next day. She was forgetful, but always remembered where the wine store was. Alcoholics are extremely crafty. They can move mountains to get their hands on a bottle.

I was overwhelmed with school, Ricky, and Mom. I simply had to unload some of my emotions. I decided to talk to Ricky about it, hoping I was wrong about his attitude. "She sat by my bed for months, and took me to millions of doctors over the years," I said one night after dinner. "I feel like I'm not doing enough for her now that she needs me. We've switched places. I get how helpless and vulnerable she must have felt after my accident. It's worse to be in the chair than in the bed. I can't stand by and watch with a smile on my face. I don't know how she did it."

I don't remember exactly what he said. I do remember what I heard—that my mother, my angel, was just a weakling undeserving of his consideration. And I do remember what I said next:

"It's over."

"What?"

"And fuck you." This time, I walked out.

A week later, I went back. I was an addict, just like Mom. He was an asshole chauvinist throwback, and I couldn't get enough. We broke up and got back together several times over the coming months. Sexual attraction (coupled with codependency) could make a person act in her own worst interests and be thrilled about it.

Linda Stein finally managed to sell the Kenilworth apartment (for $5 million). I had to move out. I found a one-bedroom rental at 401 East Sixty-sixth Street and Second Avenue. Mediterraneo, a popular Italian restaurant, was right on the corner. I had a lot of dinners there with friends, and still go with my family.

Living alone in a much smaller place, I found myself asking the big questions. I'd devoted much of the year to my conversion. But

when I was in crisis over the one human being I truly worshipped—
my mom—I found no comfort in religion or prayer. I'd made a switch
to Judaism, in part, to be with the man I loved. But he didn't love me
back enough because of the accident, which had been, arguably, an
act of God.

I'd been searching for meaning during a hard time. Something
felt missing in my heart I thought only faith could fill. But my family, for better or worse, was my true religion. We had our own history,
traditions, and laws. I wasn't so sure about God. But I was devoted
to my parents. Despite his religious nature, Ricky had no charity in
his heart for my mother, a sick woman. I started to hate myself for
wanting him at all. In one fell swoop, I gave up my boyfriend and my
religion, and made a concerted effort to find faith in myself.

CHAPTER EIGHT

Everything You Wanted to Know about Amputees (But Were Afraid to Ask)

A t my charity functions and interviews, people have a lot of questions about my prosthesis and life as an amputee. I always thought I should really write my own FAQ to answer all of the lingering questions out there. Here goes:

How Much Does Your Leg Cost?

My current legs—one for flats and one for heels—cost $30,000 each. Believe it or not, that's midrange. Prosthetic limbs can cost anywhere from $10,000 to $150,000, depending on the material, use, and style. This is why I do so much work for One Step Ahead and Challenged Athletes Foundation, both of which raise money to pay for prosthetics for children and athletes. As I know only too well, kids need at least two sets a year while they're growing. Insurance will cover only their most basic needs or will pay for one prosthetic a year, or even only one per lifetime, depending on the policy.

Insurance certainly doesn't cover cosmetics—meaning legs with realistic "skin" and "toes"—or limbs for specific purposes, like running or swimming. I campaign for children and adults who lost their limbs due to diseases or accidents, or for those who were born limbless. They deserve a fighting chance and to not be held back by their loss. Just as reconstructive surgery after mastectomies is paid for by insurance, artificial limbs for sports or aesthetics should be paid for by insurance companies. (For more information about One Step Ahead, please go to www.onestepaheadfoundation.wordpress .com and CAF at www.challengedathletes.org.)

How Often Do Adults Have to Replace Their Prosthetics?

A good one can last for years. Though with steady improvements in technology and technique, I've been known to upgrade to a better leg even if the old one is in good working order. I've had my current legs, made by Eric Schaffer of A Step Ahead Prosthetics in Hicksville, Long Island, for five years. Not only are his legs beautiful, they're very comfortable. With repairs, I could wear them for a decade or more. (A Step Ahead can be found at www.astepaheadonline.com.)

How Do You Put It On?

First I roll a custom-made silicone sleeve, like a thick condom, over my stump, a.k.a. my residual limb. And by the way, most amputees hate the word "stump." It just sounds bad. The sleeve has a pin at the bottom, pointing down. Then I put my leg with the silicone sleeve into the socket at the top of the prosthesis. The pin clicks into a hole in the prosthesis, and it is locked in place. There is no way you could pull the leg off me. You could drag me around the apartment by the leg, and it would not come off. To take it off, I press a release button (well hidden) that unlocks the pin, remove the leg, and unroll the sleeve. It takes maybe ten seconds to put on, two seconds to take off. Only the people I trust the most in the world know where the button's located. If I were in an accident and the paramedics wanted to get it off, they would have a hard time finding that button.

What Does the Leg Feel Like?

It feels like soft rubber to the touch. In terms of how it feels to wear it, it's heaven. It feels like a comfortable padded boot. I can put it on as easily as a pair of glasses and walk without pain, wear skirts, wedges, flip-flops, and look like I have two normal legs. It's a miracle. I'm grateful every day, every step, for the technology that affords me a normal life as well as the artistry that goes into making these beautiful, functional prosthetics. I'm grateful for the whole leg I have, and for my amazing "bionic" leg.

Mechanically, How Does It Work?
Does the Leg Have Joints and Springs?

The components in the leg give me bounce, like a ligament does in a real leg. My traction comes from the knee. The "ankle" isn't a flexible joint, but it bends slightly and shifts back and forth (but not side to side), making it possible for me to take a normal step.

My smooth gait also comes from years of practice. If only I'd practiced as much on the piano as I do walking with my prosthesis! I'd be playing in Carnegie Hall by now. It's also because I have a comfortable fit. Before I had my second amputation and had to endure the abrasions, I limped a lot. The equivalent would be wearing too-small shoes and walking with blisters. When I had the surgery, and the abrasions were gone, it was like throwing out the blister-inducing shoes, slipping on a pair of slippers, and walking on a cloud.

How Are Prosthetic Legs Made?

When you have a below-the-knee amputation like mine, the prosthetist takes a cast of your stump—or "residual limb," the preferred term. Then they use the cast to create a mold to build a socket for the residual limb to fit into. The artistry comes in when the prosthetist builds a foam shape of your good leg—or "sound leg" as they call it. Then they flip it, right for left, and make a foam model and fit it with a silicone "skin" on top. The aesthetics—moles, shading, veins—are designed when casting and tinting the silicone skin. It takes about two months to make a prosthesis. Other types, like sports limbs, are made differently. Each limb is custom made to each person's residual limb. No two prosthetic legs or arms are ever the same.

An above-the-knee amputation requires a more complicated prosthesis, with a mechanical "knee." It's truly a marvel of technology.

How Much Does the Prosthesis Weigh?

It's slightly heavier than my normal leg. You'd think that I'd have a muscular left thigh from lifting the prosthesis around. But my right thigh is much stronger. I favor it. I always lean and stand on my right leg. Actually, my left thigh is somewhat atrophied. I should do physical therapy to build it up but I can't be bothered. I have four kids, and too much to do.

What Kind of Exercise Can You Do?

Anything I want. I am not great at putting all my weight on my one prosthetic leg and balancing, so yoga can be a challenge. I have not gotten a running leg yet, but I am getting more and more into running and may get one soon! I can use gym machines like the StairMaster and the elliptical trainer. My preference right now is spinning class. I go three times a week to Soul Cycle (www.soul-cycle.com).

To spin, you have to click the cycling shoe into the pedal. For a long time, the teacher had to manually click my prosthetic foot into the pedal for me. I couldn't feel the click. But after a while, I got it. I spin with my flat foot. You have to stand up, sit down, go fast, go slow. I don't have a left calf muscle, after all. To compensate, my hamstring and quad have to make up the difference. I don't know exactly how I manage to pedal without an ankle joint, but it somehow works.

The real trouble at spin class, though, is sweat. My stump sweats. After forty-five minutes of spinning, sweat pours into the silicone sleeve and creates a puddle. (I could use a special deodorant to eliminate sweating altogether inside the prosthesis, but that stuff contains aluminum. See list of fears.) If I stepped off the bike like that, the sleeve would slip off. At the end of my spinning class, while everyone else is stretching, I discreetly take a T-shirt and wrap it around my knee. I release the pin and roll down the silicone sleeve. I dry the inside of it and my stump with a towel. I quickly roll the sleeve back in, click in, and I'm good to go.

This is why I always take a bike in the back row, with the wall behind me.

How High Is Your High Heel Leg?

I can wear a 3½- to 4½-inch heel. I can cheat a little up or down if I'm prepared to be off balance.

Do You Have a Swim Leg?

I use an old flat leg as my swim leg. Sometimes it stays wet for a few hours. Not a big deal.

Are Your Real and Artificial Legs Different Shades During the Summer?

No. I have my prosthesis designed a few shades darker than my good leg. In the winter, it's a nonissue because of pants and tights. During the warm months, I lay out to catch up my good leg to match the tone of the prosthesis, and then wear sunblock to prevent further tanning.

Do You Get a Pedicure on the Artificial Legs?

Of course! I go to my favorite pedicurist with my spare leg in a bag. They keep some things for me at the salon. Regular acetone polish remover actually removes the fake nail. They keep a special non-acetone remover in stock for me.

When I get a pedicure, only my real foot gets the whole treatment. But all of my fifteen toes get polish. I match the color on all three feet. First, the pedicurist polishes my real toes and whatever leg I'm wearing. While I'm drying, she takes my spare leg into the back and changes the color. Then she puts it back into the bag for me to take home. They're so sweet, they don't charge me extra for having three feet. Not once have any of my pedicurists said or done anything to make me feel uncomfortable. Though I prefer them to polish the third leg in the back and not in front of the customers. I don't want to scare them off. Once the manicurist walked out from the back carrying my prosthesis in her hand. All the patrons stared. I wanted to die of embarrassment.

Are the Toes Separated Like on a Normal Foot, or Does It Look Like a Barbie Foot?

It's not like a Barbie foot at all. The leg also has veins and capillaries, moles, and different shades. It truly is a work of art. It looks like a real human leg, not a smooth plastic doll's. It's great for my psyche to look down at my legs and see how similar they are. It's like having my own two legs. The toes are separated. Well, just the big toe. The other four are joined. The space between the big toe and the rest is the perfect width for flip-flips and sandals.

Have You Been Hit on by Amputee Fetishists?

Yes! I've been propositioned by tweet from a man who started asking me innocent questions about my leg, like, "How does it work?" and "Do you wear it to sleep?" He said he was asking for an amputee "friend." I innocently answered all questions in detail. I even sent pictures! But then he asked me to describe the stump. He asked me to send him a picture of me touching it. And that's when he got blocked. A very *creepy* and *huge* downside of being in the public eye.

How Much Does the Amputation Affect Your Day-to-Day Life?

I put on the prosthesis every morning. I have to have the skin repaired frequently. I'm pretty rough on it, so I get tears and broken nails. I'm dependent on it, like someone with bad vision relies on glasses. It seems like losing a body part—a breast, an arm, or a leg—would be among the most horrible things to endure. It has its annoyances. But human beings have an incredible ability to adapt—especially children. The new body becomes your reality. You really do get used to it. Before long, having one leg becomes the new normal.

Adult amputees do find it harder to adapt, but they do. I met a man recently who was missing his arms and legs, and he was one of the happiest guys ever. He had a beautiful wife and child. When people see him, they don't know what to do. They can't shake his hand. So he says, "Come on and give me a hug." Everyone feels at ease. He's an amazing person with an indomitable spirit. If you are a naturally affectionate, happy person, you will be that way whether you have four limbs or three. Or none. If you're a cranky, whiny bastard, then you will probably be that way after an accident or disease. Your basic personality doesn't do a 180 just because you lose a limb. You'll still be you.

The only example of my leg getting in the way of my living is having to get frequent repairs. It's a time-suck to schlepp to Long Island and wait for the fittings. Luckily, my prosthetist will let me mail the leg to him for simple repairs. I'm grateful for the skill and work that goes into my repairs. But I hate losing a day to get them or being without my prosthesis while it's in the mail.

But If You Could, Would You Have Both Legs Back?

I don't go there. No one can go back in time. I'm not going to say that the accident was a blessing in disguise. It was an accident. It changed the course of my life. Looking back at what might have been would be a waste of time. With four kids, I have no time to waste. I haven't let my leg (or lack of one) slow me down or keep me from doing anything I wanted to do. When people rewrite their own history—if I'd married that man, or landed that job, or hadn't had my foot chewed off in a barn cleaner—they're living in a fantasy world. I'm a realist's realist. I exist in the here and now. Right here, right now, I have a great life. No complaints.

Are You Discriminated Against?

A lot of people in my social and professional circles never knew I wore a prosthesis. Appearing on *The Real Housewives of New York City* was like coming out of the amputee closet. Since then, I haven't noticed any marked change in the way people treat me.

The only time I've felt a pang was when pregnant friends have an amniocentesis or sonograms. "If there was anything wrong with the baby, I would abort," they've said.

I asked, "Anything? Really? Like, say, the baby had a missing arm or leg?"

"Absolutely."

That smarts. Those people believe that their child couldn't be happy and have a full life with a missing limb. My existence wouldn't be worth having? Really? They simply don't know what they are talking about. I tell myself that if they walked a mile in my shoes, they wouldn't feel the same way.

What Other Leg Options Can You Get Besides Flat, High Heel, Swimming, and Running?

You can get a skiing leg, a dancing leg, a tap dancing leg, different legs for different sports. The sky is the limit. You can get anything you want, if you are willing to pay for it or your insurance will pay for it.

I heard Heather Mills, Paul McCartney's ex-wife, had a nightclub dancing leg. I don't know how it was different from a normal prosthesis. I danced on tables in Paris in my primitive, abrasion-maddening, hard plastic leg just fine. But if she or anyone could think up a certain kind of leg, if she has the resources, she can get it made.

What Happens If You Gain or Lose Weight? Would the Prosthesis Fit?

No, it wouldn't. And that's a huge problem. If you gain or lose ten pounds, it can affect the fit and balance of the leg. During my pregnancies, I gained forty pounds. Ideally, I would have had a pregnancy leg. But I made do with what I had. We all wake up in the morning more swollen, and as the day goes on, we shrink, especially when we're pregnant. My prosthesis was really tight in the morning. I figured out that if I slept in the silicone sleeve, I wouldn't swell as much, and I could get the prosthesis on more easily. During normal weight fluctuations, I add socks to make the socket tighter if I lose weight. If I gain, I don't wear any socks. Because of this issue, I have to be very careful about not putting on extra pounds, or eating salty food that would make me bloat.

Is It a Great Feeling to Take It Off at Night?

I do love getting into my bed and clicking it off. It just feels good to stretch out under the covers and relax. But, honestly, it's a bigger relief to take off my bra at night. My bra is more uncomfortable than my leg.

Does the Residual Leg Get Itchy or Need Special Skin Care?

It can. Fortunately, I'm not rash prone. Heat rashes can happen. Overall, the silicone sleeve protects my stump from chafing. I haven't had a single abrasion since I had that second amputation at twenty-six. I do have calluses on my knee from wearing the prosthesis. I don't slough them away, though. They give me protective natural padding.

Do You Shave the Stump?

I don't need to. I'm blond and don't have a lot of hair. The hair that grows on the residual limb is fine white baby hair and not worth risking a nick over. For others, I think shaving is not recommended because rashes can occur.

Do You Shower with the Leg On or Off?

Off. I shower standing on one leg. This is my real talent. I can shampoo, condition, lather, and scrub on one leg. If I need help with the balance, I lean on the wall for a second. In our current apartment, however, our bathtub is big and round with a curtain. I don't have a wall to lean on, so I got a little stool and sit on it in the shower.

The worst part of showering isn't having one leg. It's having kids! There's a constant parade through the bathroom. They never leave me alone in there. I don't wish I had another leg to shower. I wish I had privacy.

What Do the Kids Think about Your Leg(s)?

They think nothing of it. My kids are still very young, from eleven to two. When the time is right and their vocabulary is more advanced, I'll explain it all to the little ones. But for now, they know the basics. I had an accident when I was younger. I wear a "special leg" because I had a big boo-boo. I don't make a big deal of it, and neither do they. My older kids know some of the details. My ten-year-old stepdaughter, Veronica, came into my bedroom last night and put my prosthesis between her knees and said, "I've got three legs!" (Okay, stop thinking dirty here, guys.) She seems to have more curiosity about my leg than her siblings. When she asks me a question—a lot of the ones I've included in this chapter—I give her a clear answer she can understand. Harrison, my oldest son, is eleven, and the only time he mentions it is when I hop into the pool with my leg off. He is very protective of me and gets nervous when I swim without the prosthesis, like I might drown. It's easier to float without the heavy prosthesis, but he thinks being able to kick with two legs is safer. I explain to him that I'm perfectly fine. My five-year-old has never said a word, and my two-year-old likes to play with my silicone toenails when they fall off.

Um, Your Toenails Fall Off?

I call them my "prosthetoes." Yes, the glue that holds them on the leg wears away, and the little toenails fall off. My prosthetist sends me extra glue and spare nails. I call and say, "Yeah, hello, I need a pinky and a fourth nail. Thanks!" They send the replacement parts by FedEx, and I just do spot repairs myself. My stepdaughter Veronica thinks it's hilarious when I randomly shed a nail. We make fun of it. It's not creepy or weird to her. She loves to make fun of my foot when I get tears as well. She makes fun of me all the time. I like being the butt of her jokes. The leg is just an extension of that.

Do You Ever Use Your Leg to Get Out of Things You Don't Want to Do?

No. Well, once. I was all tucked into bed, and one of the kids called out for a glass of water. I turned to Reid and said, "I'd do it, but I've got my leg off. Sorry, honey." Reid looked at me and laughed. I think I even got an eye roll on that one.

CHAPTER NINE

Wild about Harry

Ricky and I broke up for the fifth time. My friend Lori said, "Enough with him! That guy is a jerk. You should go out with my friend Harry."

I agreed to the fix-up, but I probably wasn't in the best frame of mind to meet Harry Dubin. We had dinner anyway. My first impression of the man who would become my first husband? Only positive. Harry was a kind and real gentleman. And handsome, too, with light brown hair, sparkling eyes, a bright smile, and a solid chest in a beautifully tailored blazer. The man had taste.

I enjoyed his company and we had lots of mutual friends. I was surprised we hadn't met before. He had a worldly charm, and certainly knew his way around a restaurant. He told funny stories about his life in Washington, D.C., where he was from. I learned from Lori that he came from a family well entrenched in Washington society and that was in real estate there. (At this point, you might be thinking, *In Avivaland, every man is well to do and in real estate.* I can't explain how or why I always hooked up with guys from wealthy families. Maybe because I come from one. Like attracted like. And then like repelled like. But I don't want to get ahead of myself. . . .)

With Harry, it was not lust-at-first-sight like with Ricky. When we parted for the evening, we kissed on the cheek good-bye. I thought, *He might call again, he might not. Whatever.* I wasn't that into him. He didn't seem bowled over by me either. I went home, and telepathically begged Ricky to call. He still had a hold on me.

A month or two went by. The next time I heard from Harry, he invited me to the presidential inauguration and inaugural ball for George W. Bush in January 1997. Although I'd been to Asia and Africa and Europe, I'd never been to our nation's capital before. But for the inauguration of a president-elect I didn't support? I was flattered Harry asked me to the ball, but he was not my prince. I said, "Thanks, but no thanks."

He kept calling me, though, and we became phone friends. I ran into Harry in the city, and was pleasantly reminded of how entertaining, sweet, and funny he was. Compared to Ricky, Harry was a teddy bear, an all-American mensch. I couldn't imagine him telling any woman that she had to learn to cook or to dress a certain way. He didn't judge. His manners were impeccable. He seemed besotted by women in general. He was an inveterate flirt, but not in a creepy way. It was just part of his happy-go-lucky personality. He could talk to anyone like a lifelong friend.

My feelings for him started to change. He was someone I could relate to. I wouldn't have to try hard or be on guard with him. Harry and I started going out to dinners regularly. Afterward, we kissed on the street. It was all still very innocent and chaste, though, for months.

The turning point was when Harry invited me to a wedding in Washington. We were going to fly down and back together. We hadn't had an overnight date yet. We'd only kissed, and I wasn't ready to share a bed.

I said, "I'll go away for the weekend with you. But we've never been intimate and it'd be weird to share a room." It'd be odd for any new couple to share a bedroom so early on, but especially for me. There was the prosthesis (and bathroom) factor to consider.

He said, "Okay. I'll get you your own room."

Just like that. No fuss, no arguments. He booked two rooms at the Four Seasons in Washington for the wedding. He was just so easy! No arguments. No ego clashes. No judgments. Just smooth friendliness.

I went shopping for Washington-style clothes for the trip. I had a picture in my head of what D.C. society looked like: men in gray suits; women in conservative knee-length dresses. I picked out Jackie O–type sleeveless frocks, very conservative with high necklines. My friend Sarah took one look at them and said, "Where do you think you're going? Washington isn't *that* buttoned up. It's just like Great Neck." In the end, I borrowed a long cream Hervé Leger dress from a friend who worked with the designer.

Ricky came over to my apartment the night before our flight. We were technically over, but we still got together (for sleepovers) occasionally.

"I'm going to Washington tomorrow with Harry," I told him as we sat on the couch, holding hands.

"Don't go. I'm begging you! I need you! You can't leave me. Please, Aviva!"

Ricky sniveled when he thought another man had moved in. He'd never been so vulnerable before. And you know what? It was so not sexy. I looked at him that night, bleeding need all over the couch, and felt turned off by him. The spell was broken, finally. I went to Washington.

The wedding was beautiful. We danced and had a good time. In the back of my mind, I kept thinking, *Oh, God. I'm going to have to fool around with him*. Sarah had warned me that if I didn't, he wouldn't date me again. "There comes a time when you have to shit or get off the pot," she said.

After the party, we went to Harry's room and fooled around.

The night was sweet. Harry made me feel treasured and respected. Unlike Ricky, sex with Harry hadn't overwhelmed me, or turned me into an obsessed crazy person. I felt safe and sane with Harry, which, as I fell asleep next to him, seemed like a refreshingly healthy way to be.

As usual, I kept the leg on. Harry didn't ask about it. I was only too happy not to have to tell the story on our first night. He didn't ask about my leg on our second night either. Or the third. Or the hundredth. Not once, in our two years together, nor the ten years since our breakup. I used to think he didn't bring it up for my sake. But I came to learn he avoided *any* unpleasant conversation like the plague.

Harry liked to go out to dinner, to a bar, to parties. As his girlfriend, I went along. We made a nightly tour of Manhattan restaurants and parties. Once again, I found myself in a relationship with a man who came alive at night, like Alexandre. It was one thing to burn the candle at both ends when I was a twenty-one-year-old undergrad. But now I was twenty-seven, studying for the bar exam, and worrying constantly about my mother. I was an adult, with real responsibilities. I just couldn't keep up with Harry, too.

I woke up sick to my stomach each morning. The nausea lasted all day long. I cut out coffee, but that didn't help. For a week, the queasiness got progressively worse. I'd get hungry for a soup or salad, and order it. But as soon as it was put in front of me, a wave of nausea hit hard. I'd rush to the ladies' room.

The only possible explanation: stomach cancer.

I made an appointment with my doctor for an MRI. I couldn't study. I couldn't focus. I felt like I was wading through a fog. I described my symptoms to a friend. She said, "I spent nine months in a fog when I was pregnant."

Oh, shit. *Not* stomach cancer. An at-home test confirmed I was pregnant. Until then, I'd been so careful—almost to the point of fascism—about birth control. Knocked up? This is just not my speed. I wasn't married or even engaged. I'd envisioned a future with Harry—for a couple of months, but not the rest of my life. Was this gadfly the father of my future children? I couldn't see it. Plus, I hadn't been taking care of my health, and was taking caffeine pills to stay up late studying. I wasn't so young anymore. I wanted to have children. But it wasn't the right time.

Surgery Number Six: Termination of Pregnancy

I had to find a doctor who'd let me stay awake for the abortion. That took some doing. Finally, I found someone who'd shoot Novocain into my uterus, and let me stay awake. The abortion took ten minutes start to finish. I felt nothing. No pain, no regret. It was the obvious decision, and Harry supported it. We were totally in sync about it. Ironically, ending the pregnancy brought us closer together.

Three months later, in February 1999, my life had changed dramatically for the better. The bar exam was behind me. Whew! The stress of studying was over. Harry and I were a solid couple, and doing well. We were lingering in bed one morning, neither of us ready to start the day. Harry reached for his pants on the floor for something in his pocket. He came back up with a ring.

It was a four-karat emerald-cut diamond set in platinum. Harry had sparkling, if conservative, taste. His sense of occasion, though, was a bit dull. The delivery was so nonchalant, I wasn't sure if he was proposing, or just giving me a diamond.

"You're asking me to marry you?" I asked.

"Okay."

I paused. "Um, okay."

And we were engaged.

The wedding planning process with Jonathan had been elaborate and complicated. This time, I kept it simple. We wanted a June wedding, so that only gave me five months to pull it all together. I was crazy busy getting everything done in time, and along with an extended trip to London, the engagement period blew by in a blur. I barely had time to think.

Even if I had had the time to leisurely analyze our relationship and my feelings, I would have married Harry. I loved the guy! I adored his family, especially his grandparents. Unlike Jonathan's and Ricky's fathers, Harry's parents were very supportive of the marriage. Almost too excited. It felt great to be warmly welcomed into the clan Dubin. Harry's brother Louis had been recently married himself to a wonderful woman named Tiffany. Tiffany's family was involved in the real estate, banking, fashion, and art worlds of New York. Her mom had been a Ms. Israel and was herself a stunner and a no-nonsense woman. Her adopted father was A. Alfred Taubman, owner of Sotheby's. They were a gorgeous couple, living a life that only a select few get a front-row seat to see.

One night, Harry and I had dinner with Tiffany and Louis at Scalinatella, a great Italian restaurant on the Upper East Side. The downstairs was cavelike, as if you were dining in an Italian villa's wine cellar. When Harry excused himself, Louis and Tiffany looked at each other, and then at me. Something was up.

She said, "Aviva, we just don't understand why you're marrying Harry. We don't get it."

"We love each other," I said, taken aback.

How did they perceive me? Or, the better question, how did they perceive Harry? All I saw was a handsome, kind, great guy who came from a solid family. By asking their question, it seemed like they were giving me a vague warning. I had no idea what they were referring to. Harry would never yell at me (like Jonathan), shove me across the room (like Alexandre), or criticize me (like Ricky). I did wonder about our security: Harry didn't have a job or a killer instinct. He'd told me he had a trust fund and that money would not be an issue.

In a moment of sheer lunacy, I thought, *Tiffany and Louis are just jealous.*

The following week, an old friend called me and said, "Harry is a sweet man."

"He's the best."

"He . . . he can be a bit of an exaggerator."

"What do you mean?" I asked.

"He talks a good game, but he's kind of irresponsible."

I hung up and thought, *She's just jealous, too.*

Jennifer joined the bandwagon, raising an objection about Harry's partying. "Why does he go out every single night? And where does all that money come from?"

I wavered a bit. This was Jennifer, a long-time friend. But then again, she had two broken engagements with two gazillionaires and was desperate to get married. To continue a trend, I thought, *Jennifer—even Jennifer—is just jealous.*

Maybe my blond hair was growing backward and clogging my brain. "Jealousy" was a convenient word I used to write off any Harry negativity. I put up mental roadblocks, and wouldn't let myself think over them. If I had, I would have asked, "Jealous of *what* exactly?" Tiffany and Louis, a successful happy couple, had nothing to be jealous about. My friends didn't really either. Why settle on that one explanation? I had nothing else to hang their objections on. Harry was a great guy! Everyone loved him. I liked it that he wasn't rabidly ambitious like other Manhattan men. The high-testosterone males were ruthless and obsessed with winning. They were often self-centered and controlling. Harry was relaxed, not chased by his own vain need to prove himself. Plus, he had money. I had money. And we had each other.

A couple of months before the wedding, Harry, his sister, and I went to a function at the Waldorf Astoria to honor Billy Jean King. A woman named Aimee Mullins came on stage to say a few words. She was an impeccably dressed, beautiful blond professional athlete— and a double amputee, missing both legs below the knee. When she was on stage, I checked out her prosthetics. They looked completely lifelike. And she was wearing *heels.*

I nearly dropped my glass.

My prosthetic was pretty good. But it didn't look like a real leg, and it wasn't made for high heels. On Aimee Mullins, I saw something I didn't know existed. Later on at the event, I ran across the Waldorf ballroom and straight up to her. Breathless, I asked, "Where did you get your prosthetics?"

"Excuse me?" she asked.

I explained myself. She laughed and said, "You have to go see Bob Watts in London. He's the only one in the world who makes legs like these."

My parents and I made the journey to England and spent a week in Dorset getting fitted for a custom prosthetic. (Small-world alert: The other person at Dorset Orthopedics that week was Heather Mills, the second wife of Paul McCartney, a former client of my dad's. My father frequently told the story that when he was working with the Beatles, Linda Eastman was his assistant and a budding photographer. My father was one of the backers for the Woodstock Music and Arts festival, and made Linda the official event photographer. That was where Linda met Paul. They had a house near ours in Jamaica. I'd grown up seeing Paul and Linda and their children at Round Hill during Christmas holidays.)

Bob Watts made me two fabulous legs, one for flats and one for *heels*. Both were made of silicone, with toenails. I was going to walk down the aisle at my wedding, wearing this beautiful prosthetic, in sexy stilettos. I was over the moon. I couldn't even speak. Most little girls put on high heels for the first time at seven or eight years old. I was going to wear my first pair at twenty-eight.

Bob was as impressed with his own work as I was. He asked if I'd consider modeling my legs for an article about him in *Hello*, a British magazine. They shot a big spread with me and titled the article "A Model Patient." It was my one and only modeling moment. (Some blogger actually found this article during the airing of *The Real Housewives of New York City* season five, and accused me of lying because I denied being a model. Er, guilty as charged? It gave me a huge chuckle.)

I returned from London ecstatic and ready to get married. I was in love with my new legs, in love with Harry. Mom seemed semicoherent on the trip, too. All the cosmic spheres were spinning the right way.

Days before the wedding, Harry's mom called me. "By the way, Harry should get a job," she said.

"Okay," I said. I'd assumed he would have to work.

"He really has to get a job," she said. "Don't think he's going to make a million dollars or anything in the first year."

"No, of course not." I wasn't sure how to react. Take her weird comment as a joke? A warning? A predication? Not sure what else to do, I laughed. She did, too.

Compared to the three-hundred-person monster destination wedding I had planned with Jonathan, this one was small and elegant. We invited just family and close friends, around a hundred people. The service was at Temple Emmanuel at Sixty-sixth Street and Fifth Avenue. When the music started, my father and I were in place at the end of the aisle, ready to walk. I was wearing a beautiful sleeveless dress by Vera Wang, picked out by my mom's fashionable friend Sarah. My hair was in a low, thick Grace Kelly bun. Laura Geller, a QVC sensation, did my makeup beautifully. I took a step in my brand-new fabulous Vera Wang matching shoes and couldn't move. My dress was caught on something. The music played on, reaching the critical moment. We were behind the count.

"I'm stuck," I said.

"What?" My dad thought for a second I was backing out of another wedding.

"My dress."

Harry, at the top of the aisle, must have been confused about what was taking so long.

Dad said, "Jesus!" He grabbed the back of my dress and pulled hard. The fabric ripped off the nail it had caught on. He didn't care if it ripped off entirely. This time, I *was* getting down the aisle. Which I did. I could have seen that nail as the universe's way of trying to get me to stop and rethink the wedding. But I didn't.

Our reception was at Le Cirque, the famous French restaurant on Fifty-eighth Street and Madison Avenue. My friend Lizzy was dating the singer Seal at the time. He came to the wedding and sang to Harry and me in our hotel room afterward. That was a highlight of the night. A highlight of a lifetime!

The low point: Mom could barely function. My father was acting as her caretaker. The woman who used to organize her closets with the care and precision of a museum curator now relied on my father to plan her outfit. She'd survived wartime, and now needed help to put on her shoes. She used to be strong and articulate, and could hold a conversation with anyone. At our wedding, she sat in her chair, barely interacting. My father might've made her dance a few times. But he was just pushing her around, like dancing with a mannequin. She was there, but not there.

Harry's family threw us a second party in Washington, D.C., soon after, and invited hundreds of their friends. On this occasion, I wore a simple white sleeveless crewneck long, straight dress with no frill. We were celebrated by a different crowd. It was like having two weddings. We left from there for our honeymoon—an incredible two weeks in Italy, first Rome and then Cala di Volpe in Sardinia.

It wasn't until we got back to New York that the shit hit the fan.

The first order of business in our life as a married couple was to find jobs. Harry started looking. It was important, but not imperative.

We didn't need the income immediately. Harry was such a generous spender. He threw his credit card around at restaurants and stores. It never occurred to me, not once, to question how those bills got paid. Posthoneymoon, Harry started networking and poked around among contacts to see what positions were available in banking.

I intended to work, too. Although I had my law degree, I'd heard terrible stories about overworked associates and scandalous billing practices. I wasn't sure about wading into those shark-infested waters. I still had a sizeable amount of insurance money, despite my years in Paris, my post-Kenilworth apartment in Manhattan, and law school. After all that, I was impressed with myself that I had *any* of it left.

That July, the Dubins were staying on Nantucket. Harry, his siblings, and I chartered a small plane to fly there. I couldn't believe the size of this plane. It looked like a car with wings. The only way I could get through the flight was to take out my beads and string—I'd been playing around with some Swarovski crystal beads lately—and make bracelets. I didn't look out the window. I didn't talk to anybody. I was petrified. Keeping my hands busy helped.

We landed on the island safely. I continued to work on my beading over the weekend. When we got back to New York, I wore my bracelets out to dinners and to parties. Women would grab my wrists and say, "Where did you get that bracelet?" They begged me to sell the jewelry right off my arm. I started buying the beads wholesale, and made jewelry full time. I couldn't make it fast enough. Buyers were lining up. I actually loved the work and creative outlet.

Melissa, a friend I'd been to law school with, and I started a jewelry company together called JAM Jewelry by Aviva and Melissa. From 1999 onward, we designed, manufactured, and sold jewelry. Our legal expertise came in quite handy, actually, for contracts and negotiations with retailers. Before long, we were making serious money. In this backdoor way, my employment problem was solved.

Harry landed a job, too, at Bear Stearns. He worked for money manager Shumer Lonoff, who handled high-net-worth clients. Harry was expected to manage large portfolios of wealthy individuals. He couldn't just glom on to existing accounts, though. He had to find and bring in his own clients.

I said, "I'll be your first client." I gave the remainder of my blood money to my husband.

"Have no fear," he told me. "It'll double or triple in no time."

He went to work in the mornings. I went to work on my jewelry. We were in constant contact during the day. I might've wondered why he had so much time to chat, but I was just glad to hear from him. About six months into his employment, he came home a little earlier than usual.

"You know the money in your account?" he asked.

"Doubled already?" I asked.

"It's gone."

"All of it?"

He nodded. Harry looked ashamed and wrecked. He obviously felt worse than I did. He showed me my statement. It was empty. Not a penny left of my blood money.

"What happened?" I asked.

He rambled on about the markets for a few minutes, but didn't make a lot of sense. That was the first inkling I'd had that Harry might not have a passion for banking. Not that I knew better.

I didn't worry. I just thought, *Harry still has that trust fund.*

"Oh, well. Money comes, money goes. We'll be okay." I spent the next few hours comforting him about losing the money. I just thought the next time around—the way money was flying around Manhattan in 1999, it was like you could reach out and snatch it out of thin air—he would double it. I believed (still do) that when you marry, you trust each other with your lives. Marriage was an all-encompassing unity. As soon as we married, it wasn't "my money." It was ours to spend, invest—or lose. Everyone had ups and downs. Harry was still learning, still new at it. So he made a dicey call, and lost the money. We'd make it back. It was just material. Our health was fine. Our relationship was solid. That was what mattered. I knew for a cold fact that money did not buy happiness. Having money was nice, but it wasn't everything. I told all this to Harry that night. His spirits were buoyed enough to go out to dinner and run up a thousand-dollar tab.

I was so naive.

We dined out at Manhattan's finest restaurants. We traveled. We bought nice things. Harry paid for it all with his American Express card. Weirdly, the bill never came to the house. I assumed the bill was paid, though. Otherwise, angry collectors would have called. If Harry had shown the slightest concern about our finances, I would have sensed it. I'd seen my father's constant stress when his finances took a skid. But Harry was the same laughing generous party boy, the center of attention, who always said, "I've got it," and whipped out that card.

Since we both had jobs and I was pushing thirty, we started talking about the next steps, specifically, a bigger apartment and a baby. We were already cramped in my one-bedroom on East Sixty-sixth Street.

Dad said, "Buy. Don't rent." The purchase of our Central Park West apartment had worked out pretty well for my parents. Harry and I set our price range in the mid–six figures—ironically, the same amount as the lost blood money. I called Linda Stein and started looking for the right place to start our family. I searched and searched, from Chelsea to the Upper East Side. It was practically a full-time job. I finally found a duplex on the main floor of the apartment building Maisonette on Park Avenue. It was beautifully appointed with stunning marble, renovated bathrooms, and window treatments to die for. I was thrilled. It fit all of our criteria. I called Harry and asked him to come see it right after work.

He said, "My parents don't think it's a good idea to buy right now. They think we should rent."

"I've been looking at places for months."

"Mom only told me today."

Told him? It was a strange word choice. "I guess she knows the market."

His parents were shrewd in real estate. My dad got lucky with the Kenilworth sale, but real estate wasn't his business. If the Dubins said it wasn't a good time, then it probably wasn't. I ceded this decision to my husband.

"Okay," I said.

We came up with a new number for a rental, in the mid–four digits. I called a different broker and started looking again. I spent another month pounding the pavement, searching from Murray Hill to Morningside Heights. In the year 2000, Manhattan rentals were sky high. I was looking at places that were smaller than where we were currently living. I practically wore out a prosthesis on that apartment hunt. I finally found a sexy little duplex in a brownstone on Sixty-sixth Street between Madison and Park that came with a small backyard. Only problem: it was twice what we hoped to spend at eight thousand dollars a month. Harry loved the place, and said, "We can cover it." We signed the lease. Harry hired a decorator and used his AmEx to buy all-new furniture.

We settled into our duplex, doubling our breathing room. Having two floors, plus outdoor space, was palatial compared to the one-bedroom. I jogged up and down those stairs, loving every step, imagining our future there. It was missing only one thing—a baby. So we started trying.

Harry's mom called me every morning to chat.

"I'm concerned about Harry's job," she confided soon after our move.

"He'll be fine," I said. "Harry's a great guy!"

If our marriage and divorce were ever turned into a Broadway musical, the title would be *Harry's a Great Guy!* I believed in him 100 percent. It didn't occur to me that Harry would fumble.

His mother wasn't as optimistic as I was. A few weeks later, she said, "I don't think you should have a baby right now. You should wait until you're more settled."

We had a new apartment. I was doing well with JAM Jewelry. Harry was at Bear Stearns. Apparently we had enough money to go out every night. Why wait?

"We're pretty settled now," I said.

"Wait a bit. When Harry is more solid at work, he'll feel better about having a baby."

Now I thought Harry was talking to his mom behind my back, that he'd told her that he wasn't ready to have a baby and that I was forcing him into it. Why hadn't he told me? All along, he'd been saying he wanted a baby as badly as I did. But maybe he was just going along to make me happy. He hated confrontation or disappointing anyone.

I thought, *Okay. I can wait a couple of years.* When Harry came home from work, I never mentioned the talk with his mom. I didn't want to put him on the spot. I quietly started using birth control again. Years later, I learned that Harry and his mom had never discussed our reproductive plans. She'd made that call on her own.

Harry turned thirty-five. I took some of the profits from my jewelry line and bought him a Rolex Daytona watch. Inscribed on the back, it read, "For every hour that we live, love, and laugh together." I would have spent twice as much to please him. He worked so hard, and I adored him with a pure and open heart.

After a spontaneous night, I got pregnant. When I found out, I was afraid his mom would think I deliberately disobeyed her. When I told her the news, I swore on my good leg that it'd been a sloppy accident. She bit her lip, hard, and then congratulated us. She didn't accuse me of going against her wishes. At that point, I didn't care what she thought. I was pregnant, and thrilled about it.

Physically, though, I was miserable. From the moment I woke up to the moment I went to sleep, I was queasy. I could barely leave the house. The nausea was violent and unrelenting. Doctors diagnosed me with hyperemesis gravidarum, or severe morning sickness—the same illness Princess Kate was hospitalized for during her pregnancy. The extreme nausea endangered the health of the fetus. I tried acupuncture, massage, and healers. Nothing worked. I was too ill to make my jewelry. I hated to walk away from the business I started. I loved making my crystal bracelets. Making jewelry had given me a focus for my energies and was quite profitable. But I had to give it up to care for myself, my husband, and my mother, and prepare for my future child. All mothers—even expectant mothers—have to make tough decisions and, inevitably, have to give some things up. I missed the creative outlet, but I had to prioritize my health and family.

Melissa, still a good friend, took over the business. She renamed it and has kept it going to this day.

I struggled to keep food down for the next eight months. A one-legged pregnant woman racing for the toilet every twenty minutes was not the prettiest sight. Harry was loving and supportive, as always. I could not keep up with his desire to go out every night, and I often stayed home alone. Around month six, when I practically lived in the bathroom, Harry left Bear Stearns. He was vague about the details. "It was a mutual decision," he said. "Don't worry. I'm already lining up a new job. I'm going to work in the Broadway business with my uncle, raising money to put on shows." If he'd told me his job was to shine shoes at Grand Central, I wouldn't have cared. I was just so violently ill, the only thing I could think about was making it through the next hour.

Harrison was born on July 26, 2001. He was healthy, robust, and beautiful. Harry's parents came from Washington to the hospital to meet him. His mom offered to pay for a baby nurse, and I accepted gratefully. A brand-new mother, I didn't know what I was doing. I needed the help.

My mom and dad came a week later from Florida to meet their grandson at our apartment. Mom was really out of it. When she held the baby, she listed to the side, and seemed to forget Harrison wasn't a stack of towels. I hovered too close, ready to swoop in and catch him if she dropped the baby. Even worse, Mom didn't seem to feel anything when she held him or looked at him. She said the key phrases—"beautiful boy," etc.—but it sounded rote, rehearsed. Her eyes didn't match the words. My father confided in me that their financial situation, despite the apartment sale, was tenuous. He wanted to give Harrison so much, but he couldn't. Not right now.

It broke my heart that Dad was upset about that. The last thing he should worry about was supporting us. I was married to a grown man and I had the ability to earn income myself. Dad had to preserve his resources to help Mom. I told him, "We are fine."

It seems almost pathologically stupid that I still hadn't caught on about the "trust fund," where I thought the AmEx bills were sent, and what had made it possible for Harry to spend so much without having a job. When I asked about it, rarely, he replied craftily. His family was reserved in their comments. No one told me outright what was *really* going on. Sometimes, I'd pick up a hint. Louis and Tiffany seemed to want to tell me the truth, but that would have been a betrayal of Harry. It wasn't a conspiracy of silence. More like family protecting family.

CHAPTER TEN

Trouble with Harry

In September 2001, when Harrison was two months old, I got bronchitis and had a 104-degree fever. I was too ill to go to the doctor, which for me meant near death's door. That was when Harry's mom called and announced, "It's time to let the baby nurse go."

I barely remembered the conversation. But when Harry came home from his Broadway job, I said, "Your parents don't want to pay the baby nurse anymore. I really want to keep her for another couple of weeks, at least until I'm well."

He said, "I'll ask Mom."

I was too febrile to question it. But then I started to wonder what his mom had to do with keeping the baby nurse if we would take over paying her salary. Did Harry have to get her stamp of approval on all of our decisions, big and small? It wasn't like his mom was paying our bills, right? *Right?*

Or was she?

And just like that, the light switched on.

Harry's mom had weighed in on *everything*. Our wedding. Our honeymoon. Renting the apartment. The decorating budget. When to have a baby. How long to keep the baby nurse. I thought she was just a superinvolved mom, and that Harry, a great guy, indulged her out of habit and because he wanted to make her happy. As I lay in bed, my head burning, it dawned on me that her interest went way beyond the personal. It was professional. She kept a hawk eye on Harry's expenses because she must have been paying the bills. I remembered all the comments that people made when we got engaged. His brother and sister-in-law asking, "Why are you marrying Harry?" His own mother saying, "It's not like he's going to make a million dollars." And what about Harry's vague reasons for leaving Bear Stearns?

The only logical explanation for all of it was that Harry had no money of his own. His so-called "trust fund" was held by the First National Bank of Mom and Dad. The AmEx bills went directly to them. His investment bank job was probably set up by his family. He'd lost all of the blood money. His current job was working for his uncle. How long would that last? Harry had led me to believe that he was independently wealthy. But the opposite was true. He was dependent on his family.

The thing about taking money from your parents: it comes with strings attached. And Mrs. Dubin knew how to pull them. I realized with a sinking heart that Harry and I were puppets. I had believed his story from day one. Was I delusional? Willfully ignorant? I should have pressed him and asked more questions. I shouldn't have been so clueless about our finances. I was suddenly terrified about the future. Would Harry be dependent on his parents *forever*? I had a child to protect.

Three days later, hijacked planes flew into the World Trade Center towers. Lower Manhattan became a hellscape. Thousands of people were killed. Toxic dust rained down on the city streets. Anthrax envelopes were mailed to media outlets in midtown. The atmosphere in New York was one of shock, terror, and deep grief. People were stockpiling Cipro and gas masks, convinced another attack would happen at any moment. Manhattan was on lockdown. No traffic in or out. No subways. Sirens around the clock. Military plane flyovers rattled the windows every hour.

I was postpartum, sick, alone with Harrison, shell-shocked to learn the truth about Harry, petrified about the toxic dust, the threat of attack. The unprecedented sadness and tragedy that hit our city was overwhelming. My brother worked on Wall Street, and he ran to my home covered in soot. He could not speak for two days, and stayed in my apartment for weeks. My anxiety and hypochondria went into overdrive and didn't let up. My episodes usually lasted a few minutes to an hour. The week of 9/11, I existed in a perpetual panic attack. I simply couldn't calm down. Overwhelmed with grief over those who lost loved ones, I was terrified for Harrison and the world I had brought him into. Harry was still going to his Broadway "job," even though the entire city was in mourning and no one else bothered to show up. The world was a mess, my family was in trouble, and life was looking dismal.

I took it minute by minute. I fed the baby, changed him, and bathed him. I fed and bathed myself. I got through the day, and then the next. My body ached from being in a constant clench. The TV reports about the dead devastated me and everyone else. I couldn't stop crying. If it weren't for Harrison, I would have crawled into the closet and stayed there. I don't know how the relatives of the 9/11 victims did it.

"We have a problem," Harry announced at the end of the month, when rent was coming due. "When we rented this apartment, I told my family that it was four thousand dollars and showed them a fake lease for that amount. I got the other four thousand dollars from my grandfather. Well, my parents and grandfather somehow found out about it all. And they're pissed."

The moment of truth had arrived. Harry went on to tell me everything. The house of cards he'd built had finally toppled. His secrets were exposed. I felt sorry for him. He had to feel awful about it. But he didn't bother apologizing for lying to me from the beginning. It was beside the point. We were in crisis, and couldn't waste time on making each other feel better. We had to figure out what to do next.

I learned that I had been wrong about a few things. His parents weren't getting the AmEx bill. That went straight to his grandfather. Harry's parents hadn't known about that huge bill either. They weren't happy about it, since they also gave him a generous allowance, which his grandfather hadn't been aware of. Well, they all knew what was up now. If I'd been in their shoes, I would have been furious at Harry, too. But I was his wife. We had a son. I swallowed my anger for Harrison's sake. I asked him, "Why didn't you just tell them the truth? Why didn't you tell me we couldn't afford this place? I would have kept looking."

He just couldn't answer. There was no logical explanation. Harry, I realized, couldn't help himself. I loved how easy he was when we first started dating. But now I realized why he was so easy. To Harry, the hard truth was optional.

Harry's grandfather (also named Harry, a.k.a. Mr. Myerberg, a.k.a. Pop, as everyone called him) was ninety years old, and strong in body and will. He'd been nothing but kind to me—until that week. The man got on a train in Baltimore and came to our apartment in New

York. When he showed up, he didn't even look around. He walked into the living room and sat down in a chair. I was holding Harrison on the couch. He said, "Please remove the baby." He didn't want to conduct the ugly scene with his great-grandson present. I put Harrison in his crib. Harry and I sat next to each other on the couch.

"You two have until January First to get out of this apartment," said Pop.

The way he looked at me, he must have believed I was complicit in Harry's scheming. I can't describe the shame of it. I tried to talk to him, but he was livid. I realized that kind of thing had happened before with Harry. I bet it had happened many, many times before, going back to his childhood. The rent debacle was probably the last straw.

Although it had taken me months to find and professionally decorate this apartment, we had no choice but to find a new place quickly. I began apartment hunting with an infant strapped to my chest in a Baby Bjorn. There were a lot of new vacancies because people fled the city in the wake of 9/11. I was able to find an apartment on Eighty-sixth Street between Central Park West and Columbus. Even though the new place—a three-bedroom—cost only a thousand less than the duplex, it was a matter of principle to his family that we move. Harry had to be punished.

Harry's allowance was slashed, too. His AmEx was reined in. I learned my lesson, and started asking questions. Entitled, bratty, spoiled-wife questions like, "Do we have money for food? Can I buy diapers?"

Harry said, "Yes, yes, of course."

I went to Fairway, the supermarket in our neighborhood, to buy dinner ingredients. I waited on line with Harrison in his stroller with a chicken, some broccoli, and a loaf of bread. I got to the cashier and my debit card didn't work. Harry had promised me an hour earlier that it would. As I wheeled Harrison home empty-handed, a quiet, dark thought crept into my head: *He can't help it. Harry simply can't help it.*

Harry really was a great guy. He wasn't malicious or mean. He wouldn't intentionally hurt me or his son. He certainly hadn't set out to alienate his family and shatter the trust in his marriage. But he'd done it anyway, and would continue to do it. Harry would probably say anything to cover his ass for another five minutes. I couldn't see how I could be married to someone like that for the next fifty years.

My father called. "Aviva, we have to talk about your mother." His voice cracked when he said, "Neighbors found her in the building's elevator naked. I took away her car keys and tried to keep her locked inside. But she got out and went looking for alcohol. The cops brought her home. She was screaming at them, cursing and fighting."

My heart broke. "She has to go to rehab," I said.

"She won't do it." Whenever the subject of treatment came up, Mom flew into a violent flailing rage. Dad and I talked constantly about having her committed involuntarily.

"Is it really up to her?" I asked. Mom couldn't make rational decisions. She had alcohol-induced dementia. She didn't recognize people and places.

"Well, I won't do it either." Dad didn't have the heart to force her into rehab. He'd done it before, and spent a fortune. As soon as she got out, she started drinking again. If the patient didn't want to be there, treatment was a pointless exercise. "Can you come down?" he asked.

My father hardly ever asked for anything. But he wanted my help. I hadn't told my parents what was going on in New York with the Dubins. Dad knew we moved, but not the reason why. I couldn't bring myself to tell him I didn't have money for a plane ticket to Florida.

"As soon as I can," I said.

Harry's mother and I still chatted almost every day, making nice, keeping up a facade of civility. "Harry needs to send monthly reports to his investors at the Broadway job," she said one morning.

"Okay," I said. "I'll tell him." I knew my role now, no need for double-talk. I was responsible for keeping Harry on track, but in classic Dubin indirect style. The uncle had complained about Harry's performance to his mother. She told me. And then I had to tell him. I had no idea why his uncle and boss didn't tell Harry himself.

When he came home, I did my duty. "Your mother told me to tell you to send the investors' reports."

"Yes, yes, I'll do it," he said.

A cut in allowance didn't stop Harry from going out every night. He simply couldn't stay cooped up. He went stir crazy, especially when the baby was fussy. I couldn't stomach spending money I now knew wasn't ours, and stayed home with Harrison. My son was a more entertaining companion than a bunch of barflies. But Harry had no problem leaving us behind to hang out at restaurants and bars. It was his compulsion. He needed to socialize. A baby and a wife weren't enough for him. My options were to invite guests to our apartment and cook every night—not going to happen—or just stand aside as he raced out the door to get his people fix.

The news reported that a rapist was terrorizing our neighborhood. I couldn't stay home by myself knowing that. Harrison and I joined Harry for dinner at a restaurant. After dinner, though, I'd had enough. The baby needed to go to bed. "I'm going to stay for a bit longer," he said. "Just go home without me."

"Are you sure the windows are locked?" I asked.

The rapist's MO was to enter apartments with open windows and attack victims in their own homes. We lived on the second floor, with scaffolding built right up by our windows. I was convinced the rapist would target our apartment.

"I'm sure they're locked," he said.

"Can you bring us home to check?"

"I checked before we left," he insisted. "The windows are closed and locked."

When Harrison and I got home, the windows were wide open.

That was *my* last straw. My husband was beloved by all his friends. He was the kindest, most generous, fun-loving party boy in New York and Washington, D.C. But he was never going to stay home with me and the baby. He seemed to have a problem with consistency. Being married to this Great Guy, I would never feel safe and protected. Danger and uncertainty would always find their way in.

Still, I wasn't quite ready to end it. We had a son together, and I felt obliged to save my marriage. We tried counseling, as a couple and individuals. At one of my sessions, the shrink asked me flat out, "Can you spend the rest of your life this way?"

I said no.

"Get out."

I hung on. I'd done some reading and thought I'd found an underlying cause for Harry's behavior, something that could be solved.

Anyway, I took my case to his parents, asking them to help me help Harry.

His father said, "He can get help, but it has to be here. I'm not supporting another family in New York. If you come to Washington, I'll give you a car and you can live in one of my condos."

"No way," said Harry. "I'm not moving to Washington."

I was relieved. I didn't want to leave New York. But less than a month later, Harry agreed to take a job in his brother Louis's company in Washington. He commuted to the capital for the weekdays—living in a condo—and came back to New York to see Harrison and me on the weekend. He insisted I remain right where I was. He did not want to get stuck in D.C. When he got home on Friday night, he basically said hello to us, gave us a courteous hour of his time, and then went out. I spent most of my time alone with the baby, fretting about the future. This was not a marriage. I might as well be a single parent.

I might be better off as a single parent.

My shrink was right. I had to get out.

Divorce is a serious matter. My situation had become unlivable. I was able to tolerate everything except the lying. I could have overlooked the financial tangles, the partying, the absences. But I could not bear the lying. I just reached the point when I knew it was over.

My first step was to move *again* to a cheaper apartment on the East Side, a place I could probably afford on my own if I could save some money first. Next, I had to get my confidence back. I flew to Florida to help my dad, to tell my parents that I was going to leave Harry—and to get a boob job. Upward and onward!

Why did I do it? I convinced myself that if I didn't enhance my body, I wouldn't be able to attract another man. Who would want me? A one-legged, over-thirty, soon-to-be divorcée with a baby, no money, and small tits? My whole life, the question "Will she ever find a husband?" had been asked about me. Well, I had, and it was a disaster. I'd lost all that money, my youth, and my pride. I was in such a dire state, I thought the only way I would be able to support Harrison and myself was by finding a new man. I acted out of insecurity and emotional desperation.

Surgery Number Seven: Breast Augmentation

I asked Dr. Leonard Roudner of Coconut Grove if I could be awake for my boob job. That idea was shut down. I was in a weak state and let them talk me into general anesthesia. I asked him beforehand if anyone had ever croaked on the table.

He said, "Come on, none of that."

I survived and woke up with 29D breasts, up from a 29B. I had the boobs done in Florida because it was cheaper and Dr. Roudner was known to be the best in the world. In hindsight, I should have stayed in New York. The northern doctors made breasts smaller, more fashion friendly. Miami boobs were just too big.

Eleven years later, I regret that surgery. My prosthetic boobs are my cross to bear. They remind me of that horrible time, plus they don't even look good anymore. I breast-fed two more children with them, and they've become huge and saggy. The term "rocks in socks" comes to mind. My bras are like iron maidens and far more bulky and uncomfortable than my prosthetic leg. Soon I'll work up the courage to have the implants removed—if I can just find someone to do it while I'm awake!

After the surgery, woozy and in pain, I went back to my parents' house with Harrison. I crawled into bed and lay down. My mother came in and sat in a chair next to me.

"What do you think you're doing here?" she asked.

"I'm taking a nap," I said.

"Not in my house! Get the fuck out of here! How dare you act like you belong here! You're a disgusting whore!" she screamed.

She didn't recognize me. "Who do you think I am?" I asked.

"You're George's whore," she said. "Don't act innocent with me. I know you're fucking my husband." Her beautiful face was contorted into an ugly mask of hate. She kept on yelling at me, calling me filthy things, until she tired herself out and left. Who was this person who had invaded my mother's body? The woman I knew was the picture of elegance and grace. Cursing? Yelling? My real mother was gone.

I just started crying. It was all too much. Everyone I loved was spiraling downhill as quickly as I was. After a night and day of crying, boobs aching, I knew I couldn't go on like that. Self-pity helped no one. I took my Advil and hauled my swollen boobs out of bed.

"What can I do?" I asked my dad. He'd been caring for my mother by himself. She screamed at him, too, saying hateful things.

"Just stay for a while," he said.

I rode out the summer in Florida taking care of Harrison and my mom. Some days, she knew who I was; others, she didn't. It was a rough couple of months. But I was glad I did it. When Mom was lucid, she was still my angel. I missed her the most when she was herself. Harry visited occasionally that summer. It was awkward and not at all affectionate.

In the fall, I went back to New York to hire a lawyer.

I called Barry Slotnick, a criminal defense attorney icon. He represented subway vigilante Bernhard Goetz in the '80s. He'd also handled some high-profile political trials, as well as celebrity divorces.

He'd won millions in settlements. Rightly so, his services didn't come cheap. The initial retainer was twenty-five thousand dollars. I sold my engagement ring to pay for it.

The first thing he told me was that it was okay for me to leave the apartment because Harry had no income. When I told him about the credit card bills and rent amounts, he quickly changed his mind. I had to stay. I didn't love the idea of sharing an apartment. But in New York, it was common for couples who hated each other's guts to sleep in the same bed throughout their divorce so one or the other couldn't get the upper hand and sue for abandonment. He also told me to hire a detective so I could catch Harry cheating and have grounds for divorce. I did hire someone, and got what I needed. It wasn't a terrible blow. Cheating, schmeating. At that point, I'd detached emotionally.

Harry was commuting back and forth to Washington. When he was in New York, he kept up his same old routine of going out every night and often, drinking. After the summer with my mom, alcohol disgusted me more than ever. Harry slept on the couch. We barely talked and didn't do anything together. He must have known I was planning to file for divorce.

It was time for us to face the reality that our marriage was over. I invited myself along to dinner with him. He was surprised, but acted happy that I'd finally agreed to join him. We sat down at the table at a burger restaurant on First Avenue. Before we'd even ordered drinks, I said, "We need to separate."

He looked upset. And then genuinely devastated. My turn to be surprised. We'd barely interacted for months. I think he really wanted to have a family and to love us. But he was just not able. I was crying.

"I'll move to my brother's," he said, "and I'm taking Harrison."

"Harry, you know I'm a great mother," I said. "And you are not the type of guy who would take a child away from his mother."

In fact, he never tried. I was the only parent Harrison really knew. Harry was always "working" in another town, or out on the town. He didn't have the patience or attention span to care for a baby. Harrison was only one and a half. He needed his mommy. Plus, Harry wanted to be free. Custody of his son would infringe on his socializing.

The crux of our divorce was not going to be custody. It was going to be about money. All those years of pretending money wasn't important and didn't matter, or that it would just magically appear, had finally caught up with me. The reality was, I needed money to care for my child. I didn't have a job, and couldn't find one overnight if I tried. I was thirty-one, and had worked in an office—that estate planning insurance firm—years ago. I had two advanced degrees, but I had not worked or earned income in years. How did that happen?

Harry lawyered up. Papers were filed. Hiring Barry Slotnick was one of the smartest decisions in my life. He commanded respect in a courtroom and made a great case for me. The legal ins and outs were complicated and exhausting. A law school graduate, even I found them tedious to follow.

First, we separated. Before the divorce was settled, the judge would award me interim support in the meantime. Since Harry did not have an actual income, the monthly support amount would be based on what was called "imputed income." That was calculated by tallying up Harry's expenses, all those dinners and trips and clothes and random charges his family had been floating to him. Barry had to subpoena the AmEx bills. I had no idea how big they were until the judge awarded me a generous interim amount partially for alimony and partially for child support.

Naturally, I was happy about it. However, with no assets, a hefty rent, and Manhattan prices for sitters, taxis, food, clothes, and diapers, the monthly amount would get used up fast. And the legal fees had only just begun.

"We're probably years away from a final settlement," Barry warned.

I was, as per my style, a bit of a pain in the ass, and I asked him a thousand questions about what was to come. He looked at me and said, "The worst thing that can happen is that you will just have to get a job."

I asked, "Are you hiring?"

He wasn't. Not me, anyway.

Harrison turned two. He'd lived in three apartments in two years—four counting my parents' in Miami. His father was the man who passed through for a bit of time on the weekends. Harrison was my life. I took extreme care over every article of clothing, every morsel of food, every bath, every diaper. Harrison and I were together 24/7.

Yes, I could have tried to find a job. But that would have meant leaving Harrison in someone else's care. I did not have a relative to leave him with if I worked. I simply couldn't bring myself to let him go. The only consistent, reliable element of his life thus far had been me. I was on edge when Harry took Harrison for a weekend.

"I don't know how I'm going to live without him," I said to my friend Kelly.

"Jesus, Aviva, it's two days," she said.

During Harry's custody weekends, stories would filter back to me. Harry was out on the town as usual, until late, bragging to the last person at the bar what a great dad he was. Meanwhile, his son was left in a hotel room with a baby-sitter. It was all I could do not to storm the place and take my son back home. Nonetheless, I knew Harry was doing the best he could, and he was always a loving father.

Barry was right. It took another two years of going back and forth with our lawyers to finally settle the divorce on the same terms of the interim award. We met at a law office and sat in the conference room at the firm Blank Rome. I was with my lawyer, and Harry was with his. We signed our divorce decrees, shook hands, and that was that. Harry and I had no ill will. We even got in a cab together and went uptown. He promised me that if the settlement wasn't enough, that he could always give me more. It was just so *friendly*.

I heard later that Harry told people he was paying double the actual amount.

On the last day of our marriage, I felt the same way about Harry as I did on our first. He was a good, easygoing, kindhearted man. Our time together hadn't been easy, but we got Harrison out of it. I would do it all over again for my son.

CHAPTER ELEVEN

It Only Takes a Second, Part Two

Harrison and I went to Bed Bath & Beyond on Sixty-first Street and First Avenue for new towels. In high glam mode, I wore sweatpants with no makeup, my hair in a messy ponytail. Plus, I was grouchy. Have you been to BB&B on a Saturday morning as a single mom? It would put anyone in a bad mood.

I took my pile to the register to check out. While I was paying, Harrison, two and a half at the time, wandered over to a little girl in the next line. Seeing my son make fast friends made me smile. My frame of mind brightened. I bought two lollipops by the register, grabbed my bag, and went over to the two kids. I knelt down and gave a lollie to each child.

The girl looked over at a man in line. Her father? He nodded, and she unwrapped the candy. Apropos of nothing in particular, the man said, "It's tough being a new single dad."

What? Single? I flung my hair back and said, "Oh, I'm single, too."

I took a closer look at him. Turned out, he was *nerdy*. He wore pleated khaki shorts with a cell phone clipped to the belt and a tucked-in T-shirt. If he'd been wearing white socks with Teva sandals, it would have finished the look. I took him for a professor or an engineer. He had a handsome face. Dark hair and eyes, perfect teeth. He looked like a nice Jewish guy. His body was just my type. Tall, built, dark, and masculine.

"Can I have your number?" he asked.

Whoa, not so nerdy after all, I thought. He had plenty of confidence for a guy with his phone clipped to his belt.

It'd been several months since Harry and I separated, and over a year since we'd stopped having any kind of real marriage. I'd been focused on Harrison (with occasional trips to Florida to help with my mom), and had barely dated. I'd hoped my boob job would make an impact when I was ready to jump into the dating pool. But I hadn't yet dipped a toe in the water. I was in no rush to start that up again.

And then, in all of five seconds, this guy not only caught my eye, he got my number. I scribbled my name and contact info on my Bed Bath & Beyond receipt, and gave it to him. But he didn't call me. I was surprised, but not disappointed. Like I said, I wasn't all too eager to date. A few weeks later, I came home and found a note left for me in the lobby of my building.

"Hi, Aviva," it read. "This is Reid Drescher. We met at Bed Bath & Beyond. I lost your number. Please call me."

The guy had tracked me down, come to my home, left a message, and asked me to call him. I could take that one of two ways: (1) he was a stalker, or (2) he was smitten and aggressive. I thought, *How many Jewish stalkers are there?*

Then again, if there was only one Jewish stalker in the world, I'd be the woman to attract him.

The note made me genuinely curious about this Reid Drescher. He'd gone to some lengths to find me. So I called him. We went to a Mexican restaurant called Maya on First Avenue and 63rd Street, just a few blocks from my building. He picked me up, and we walked over together.

The number-one rule for first dates: don't talk about your ex.

We broke that rule before our drinks arrived.

"So . . . you're a single dad?" I asked.

"And you're a single mom," he said.

That was it. We were off and running. For the entire evening, we hashed over our respective divorces-in-progress. From the sound of it, Reid and his wife just weren't getting along. They seemed like a normal couple that had grown apart. His daughter, Veronica—whom I'd met—was one and a half. For her sake, he and his wife promised each other to have an amicable divorce. They were just getting started on working out a settlement.

I was six months into my settlement battle. What I'd noticed among my friends was that divorce brought out the worst, even in the finest people. Reid's divorce seemed exceptionally tame. He spoke respectfully about his wife. Reid had discretion and great manners. He was careful in his descriptions. I wasn't quite sure why he and his wife were splitting up. Reid went on to tell me about his own brokerage firm, which he started at age twenty-nine. He was obviously self-made, highly intelligent, and a workaholic.

I told him about my jewelry business, and the saga about Harry. Unlike my friends who all had Harry fatigue, Reid hadn't heard the story before. I had a new person to bounce it off of, and see if it was as crazy as I thought. I put it all on the table, and half expected Reid to get up and leave me alone there. After all, Reid was very normal.

When I finally stopped talking, he said, "Wow, that is really complicated." And then he took a big bite of his enchilada.

This was a man who didn't scare easily. *Yeah, but how would he react if I showed him my leg?* I wondered. He'd had enough for one date. I'd spring the leg on him if we had another.

When the conversation lightened up and we spoke about entertainment, it came up that Reid's first cousin was Fran Drescher. Interesting. *The Nanny* was hilarious, and was set right here, on the Upper East Side. I was sharing nachos with Fran Drescher's cousin. Reid was low key about it and unimpressed. We shared a coolness regarding celebrities. I was happy he didn't have the same nasal tone and accent. It suited sexy Fran, but for a guy . . . not so much.

He and Fran had plans to see a *Raisin in the Sun* revival starring Sean Combs on Broadway. He had an extra ticket and invited me to come. It was our second date. "I'll send a car service to your place," he said. "You go pick up Fran and then come get me."

I'd met many celebrities in my life. But being alone in a town car with Fran Drescher for twenty blocks intimidated me. Not because she was a celeb. I hoped she'd like me for Reid's sake. If she hated me, she could tell him, "Dump her. She's a loser."

The car pulled up to her building on Central Park West. Fran saw me and waved. (I told Reid to tell Fran to look out for a blonde in an orange dress. It was by Celine and I still own it.) She was wearing a tight V-neck dress in a bright color. She let herself into the car, sat down, and turned to me. "Hi, I'm Fran," she said. She asked how I met Reid, and I told her the BB&B story. She put me at ease immediately. We kept laughing the whole ride. Her voice alone—a toned-down version of her character's—cracked me up. We talked about the play, which I'd studied in drama class at Vassar. She was a Broadway connoisseur and we compared notes on musicals and our favorite theaters. Fran was cerebral and a bit spiritual, too—a fascinating, insightful, funny woman. She was nothing like her character on television. Her sophistication, intelligence, and plans to make the world a better place were inspirational. Fran was a cancer survivor and was going to use her fame and experiences to eradicate cancer through early screening for women. We could have kept gabbing all night, but we had to shut up when the curtain rose.

The performance was brilliant. Afterward, Fran and her friend went off to a party. Reid and I had dinner at Mediterraneo, my old favorite restaurant. It was warm so we sat outside. Meeting Fran, great theater, a delicious meal, and a tall, kind handsome man across the table—it was truly a magical night, one for the books.

Our conversation on that night delved further into our personal histories. Reid grew up in Queens. His father was also an accountant with his own firm. After his parents' divorce, Reid moved with his mother to Great Neck, Long Island, which is why he didn't share Fran's distinctive Queens accent. He went to the University of Miami, following his older sister and brother there. His first job out of college was at Prudential Securities. Within a few years, Reid was poached by Paine Webber as a top producer, and shortly thereafter, started his own stockbrokerage and investment banking firm called Spencer Clarke. He was successful, and took care of his mother. He hired his father to be the CFO of his company. Reid had been given nothing, and gave back to his parents everything he could.

We jumped in our chairs at all the things we had in common. Accountant fathers. Great Neck, which I knew well because of Ricky. My prosthetics office was near there, but I didn't tell Reid that. He lived in Miami during college, within ten miles of my parents' house.

He was wonderful, but too normal. I didn't trust it. I had a skewed prejudice against a normal upbringing like Reid's. The biggest drama he had known was his parents' relatively friendly divorce. He had done classic suburban things, like get a fake ID, go to weekend keggers on someone's deck, and sneak into the movies. Always ambitious, he made a lot of money in the summers selling ice cream on the beach. During college, he partied at frats and cheered for the football team. He had a steady job, and regular relatives who, for example, went to a doctor when they were sick. I had grown up in a nutty, New York City, Woody Allen–type family. At times, I felt like a damaged person myself. I'd attracted and been attracted to other damaged people and seen one relationship after the next blow up in my face.

Reid was admirable, sane, calm, self-made, and exactly the type of stable man I *should* be in a relationship with. This man could make me feel safe. Being with him would be the smartest thing I ever did for myself, and for Harrison.

So, naturally, I resisted it. It wasn't so much that I didn't think I could handle normal. But I didn't think Reid could handle me. I decided to test his mettle.

"You should know that I have only one leg," I said suddenly, interrupting him.

"*What?*" he asked.

"I had an accident when I was little, and lost my leg. I wear a prosthesis from the knee down." I studied his face. Would he grimace, gag, or say, "Check, please!"

"*Really? Can I see it?*" He lit up with curiosity.

"I don't usually lift up my skirt until the fourth date, but okay." I raised my hem to just over the knee. Reid leaned forward and touched the prosthesis. While he felt up my leg, I studied his face.

Not a hint of revulsion or horror on it. The opposite. He seemed fascinated, but not in a creepy way. He was just a curious person. I'd never been so brazen about showing my leg to a man before. And, when I did get around to it, none of my previous boyfriends had reacted with open wonder. They'd been accepting, especially Jonathan. But Reid actually seemed impressed by me and viewed my leg as if it were nothing more than a double ear piercing.

That night, Reid walked me home. My true confession didn't send him running for the hills. He was still interested. We didn't kiss good-bye, but I really liked him. He was just such a good person. Not a great guy in the Harry mold. Reid seemed to have moral fiber and was the kind of man any woman would be thrilled to be with.

A few days later, we met for coffee. And I broke up with him.

I played the "bad timing" card. "Both of us are going through divorces," I said. "I don't think it's a good time for us to start something."

Reid looked at me with sad puppy dog eyes—the same ones our five-year-old son uses on me now. When I saw his crushed expression, I knew I'd made the right decision. He wore his heart on his sleeve. He was vulnerable, and I would only complicate his life.

"Let's be friends," I said.

I'd pushed him to prove himself by showing my leg. He had, and passed with flying colors. We'd been on two great dates, and seemed to be beginning a comfortable relationship. But I couldn't relax into it. I bristled against it. Instead of staying in the city and letting things develop with Reid, I ran scared. Harrison and I moved to Florida for the summer.

It's amazing he didn't hate me.

*　　*　　*

It only took a second to meet Reid. But it took longer for us to become a couple. He would become my prince in good time. But I still had some frogs to go through that summer.

First there was the Italian playboy. He was the husband of the daughter of the ex-president of a Latin American country. Tony's father-in-law had been a dictator who allegedly killed political rivals. Tony and his pregnant wife lived in Miami for years until they had a major fight, and she flew back to her country for the birth of their baby. Tony stayed in Miami alone. I met him on the beach. He lied and told me he was getting divorced. I only went out with him twice. The second date, I drove to Tony's place and could have sworn a car was following me, but I wasn't sure. Tony called me and told me to turn around, and that we should meet back at my place. We made out that night, but nothing serious. I was too spooked by the car tailing me.

The next day, someone called my parents' home number. My father picked up. The voice said, "Do you know that your married daughter was with the president of _____'s married son-in-law last night?" The caller gave Dad some graphic details and threatened him to make me stay away from Tony.

Dad went from zero to sixty in five seconds and started screaming into the phone. "Don't you fucking call this house again, you fucking piece of shit, or I'll slice your head off!" He didn't take kindly to threats or assaults on our family. We decided that the dictator had spies in Miami. They were tracking Tony's movements and interactions on behalf of the pregnant wife. That one phone call was more than enough to make me back off.

Next was the French restaurateur, Pierre. He asked me out one night when I'd gone to one of his restaurants for dinner. He was a bit older than me, and seemed to know everyone in Miami. I was flattered by the attention, and we went on a bunch of dates. It reminded me, only in a good way, of my relationship with Alexandre in Paris, not only because they were both French. Pierre was charming and funny and in the nightlife business. We kissed a few times. But I felt nothing. It just wasn't going to happen. We're still friends, and I always go to his restaurants when we're in Miami.

I also dated this successful American real estate man (yes, another one). We went on three dates and he was smitten. He begged me to go away with him and we made out after each dinner on the street. On the fourth date at the end of dinner I said to him, "I think you should know that I had an accident when I was six and I lost part of my leg." His face dropped. And he asked for the check. He took me home. No makeout session and he never called me again. I don't have contempt for him at all. We all lose attraction to people for superficial reasons. But given the situation, I think he should have faked it for another date to spare my feelings. He has said to mutual friends, "I just couldn't deal with the leg."

In July, my friend Shoshana and I were on the beach playing with Harrison, and my phone started ringing. I saw the caller ID. It was Reid. I hadn't spoken to him since that coffee breakup. Was he a glutton for punishment?

"Who's that?" asked Shoshana.

"Just some guy in New York."

"What guy?"

"His name is Reid. He's an investment banker, super nice. Normal. Dark hair, dark eyes. Pretty cute, with a good body. He's Jewish, separated. He's got an adorable daughter. We went on a couple of dates, and he was incredibly cool about my leg."

"He sounds great! Call him back."

Shoshana kept nagging me until I called. Reid and I talked for a minute. It was a good conversation, and I was glad to hear his voice. But it wasn't an epiphanic moment.

In August, a hurricane bore down on Miami. The weather forecasters were going nuts, calling it the Storm of the Century, describing it in biblical proportions. Some friends with a plane offered to fly Harrison and me back to New York. I wanted to go. Government officials were encouraging residents to evacuate. Our place was in the heart of the red zone. I was ready to pack my bags and get my son out of there. But my father would not leave Miami. George was antiestablishment. He didn't believe in mainstream medicine, the political system, or the Weather Channel.

"It's corruption and bullshit," he said. "They're making it up to sell advertising. I'm not leaving my home over a made-up doomsday storm."

The more the newscasters screamed, "Run for your lives!" the deeper Dad dug in his heels. What scared me even more than riding out a hurricane was abandoning Mom and Dad to fend for themselves when it hit. I had to stay. My brother was around then, too. He had been working in Miami for several years for Harry's brother Louis. And even during and after my divorce, he kept that job for quite a while. We agreed to hunker down and get through it together. Dad was adamant that it'd be no big deal. Mom didn't know if it was day or night, much less care about the oncoming hurricane.

I was nervous. I went into my room, very unsettled. And then I got a text. "Are you okay?"

It was Reid. He was the only person from New York who'd figured it out and realized I was in the eye of the storm. Reid was thinking about me, and he was concerned.

I was happy to see his caller ID, and called him right back. We talked for hours. I was touched and soothed, and felt other emotions I wasn't accustomed to. I felt protected. His voice alone removed my fear and relaxed me. By the end of our talk—I didn't want to hang up—I was laughing off the storm, and said, "Bring it on." Reid was the human equivalent of a bulletproof vest.

As it turned out, Dad was right. The hurricane was a washout, a tempest in a teacup. There was hardly any damage to property, and zero casualties. I could have stayed in Miami for another couple of weeks. But I was itching to return to New York.

Harrison and I got back into the rhythm of the city. He started nursery school. For the first time since he was born, I had some free time. I started hanging out with Reid—as friends. During the week, in the evenings, he took me to SoHo House, a downtown club where he was a member. On the weekends, we met up with Harrison and Veronica, who got along so well together. Reid and I weren't dating as much as play dating.

Veronica was a baby still, barely two, an adorable ragamuffin with sweet eyes and wavy hair. Harrison had white hair and chubby cheeks. Seeing the two of them playing on the floor together was adorable. She was just so cute. I felt a maternal pull toward her. The four of us became a kind of family. Reid and I took them to plays, museums, the park, and art festivals all around the city. I was thrilled to have someone to do kid stuff with after taking Harrison around alone for years. I scoured the papers for activities for us. It was tremendous fun. Reid didn't try anything physical with me. We just kissed on the cheek good-bye after each play date.

Reid and Veronica always came to our apartment. He was still living with his soon-to-be ex-wife. Their apartment was on the market. Until it sold and their divorce was final and they divided the profit, they both had to stay put. Both of their lawyers advised them that the first one to move out, or abandon the marriage, would lose the apartment value and custody of the child. He and his estranged spouse, Jane, slept in the same apartment but in separate rooms.

Reid kept me apprised about his divorce. It escalated steeply while I was in Miami, with hurled accusations and vicious arguments. The venom and fighting were far worse than anything between Harry and me. They had explosions over meaningless petty stuff, like taking a bite out of the cookie dough in the fridge. Reid's spending every weekend with a separated mom who had a son close to Veronica's age certainly didn't improve matters.

Once I phoned Reid at the office and he said, "Aviva, you can't call me during work."

I was shocked. Harry used to call me dozens of times a day to take a break from his bank job. Reid, however, worked hard at work, which was a highly attractive quality. But we were just friends. Divorce buddies. That was it.

One afternoon he and Veronica were leaving my apartment after a particularly nice day together. The kids had just finished a half an hour of jumping-on-the-bed fun. I walked him to the door. Reid asked, "So, are you falling in love?"

I turned purple. Then he quickly added, "With Veronica?"

It was one of the most embarrassing moments of my life. Unbeknownst to me, my feeling had been changing from like to love. He must have sensed it, and put me on the spot. I was exposed and at a disadvantage. I had to tamp down those feelings quickly.

At our next play date, I asked him, "So, what's your type? Because I have a friend I want to fix you up with."

He frowned. "I like petite girls."

Petite? I was five ten. Well, that answered that.

"My friend Lori's small. She's single and would be the perfect wife for you."

Reid acted peevish for the next hour and left early with Veronica. I was so blonde I honestly had no idea why he got so angry.

He cooled on me for a week or so. But then we were back to being a faux family again. We met up on Sunday for breakfast at a coffee shop with the kids and a baby-sitter. The kids were running around the place, leaving Reid and me, and the sitter, at the table. Reid launched a complaint. "I'm spending all this time with you, but I'm not moving on with my life," he said.

I asked, "Do you mean, like, S-E-X?"

He laughed. "Aviva, I think the baby-sitter can S-P-E-L-L."

She nodded, sipped her coffee, and said, "Yes, I C-A-N."

It felt like an ultimatum. If he wasn't going to have S-E-X with me, he wasn't going to spend so much time with us anymore. I started to get nervous. I did not want to be without this responsible, stable, calm, kind, protective, wonderful man.

Reid went to California for a week on a business trip. I had a lot of thinking to do. Neither of us was divorced yet. I was still wary of getting deeply involved. Now that we were such great friends, sex could bring us extremely close, which was scary enough, or it could destroy the friendship we had. My two closest friends who knew Reid, Krissy and Genifer, convinced me to go for it. When he came back from California, it was late October. He had a Halloween party to go to that night, and met me first for a drink. He had a ghost mask with him.

"We should give this a try," I said. "But we're not going to be exclusive. We are never going to get married. And we'll always be friends first."

He smiled and asked, "Can I kiss you now?"

Purple face again. After months of being friends, the sexual turn was too sharp. I said, "Go to your party. We'll kiss next time we see each other."

And that was exactly how it happened. We went on a date—no kids—and then came back to my place. We finally kissed and moved from the couch to the bedroom. Slowly, we got undressed and climbed under the covers. Reid rocked. (I would write more here but my children may Google this.)

During our next encounter, as I entered the bed, Reid asked, "What're you doing?"

"I'm . . . isn't it obvious? I'm getting into bed."

"You left your leg on."

As I had every single other time I'd had sex. "I like to keep it on."

"Absolutely not," he said. "We don't need it."

To this day, I don't know if he said that for his pleasure or mine. The prosthesis had always been like wearing a big boot in bed. I'd never once even tried to take it off, or thought how rubbing up against it during sex would affect my partner. Reid was honest with me. And I was brave for him. I unlocked my leg, rolled down the sleeve, and was naked, really and truly naked, with a man for the first time in my life.

It was a revelation. I felt free, lighter than air. From that point on, when I got in bed with Reid, I'd just fling my leg off.

The sex was always amazing. After two weeks of having the time of our lives together, I said, "Remember when I told you we were going to date other people and that I didn't want to marry again? Well, I changed my mind."

It was all he needed to hear. Several months later, Reid called the kids into the living room, and presented Harrison and Veronica with matching kiddie rings.

"These are brother and sister rings," he said.

Harrison really got into it. He proposed siblinghood to Veronica. "Will you be my sister?" he said. Veronica let him put the ring on her finger and she returned the favor. I died of sweetness right there. After their little ceremony, they went off to play.

Then Reid took another ring out of his pocket. This was no kiddie ring. It wasn't a big honking diamond either, which was a relief. I wasn't a fan of diamonds. They make other women really happy, and that is great for them. Diamond engagement rings hadn't worked out too well for me the last two times.

Reid's ring was from the jewelry store Seaman Schepps. It had a center gemstone of yellow kunzite, with yellow citrines on each side. It was chunky, cool, and fun, not a serious, staid, predictable diamond. I loved it.

Reid got right to the point. "Aviva, will you marry me?" he said in the same no-nonsense voice he'd used to ask for my phone number at Bed Bath & Beyond nearly two years earlier.

I said, "Yes! Just as soon as I'm not married to someone else, I'll marry you!"

The ring fit perfectly. The yellow stones were instantly calming.

It hit me that the greatest thing Reid could give me was a sense of calm. He represented stability, and security. What turned me off initially was what attracted me the most in the end. Along with being the first man to see me completely nude, he was also the first I called a friend before a boyfriend. He was the first who wanted to protect me. I felt like I was in high school all over again, like the luckiest girl in the world. Not only was I marrying a handsome, kind, brilliant man, but he was so unspoiled, so different from anyone I had ever known. He was a real man with elegance and level-headedness. He put us all first and still does unconditionally. This was not a man who would travel a lot, or take Vegas trips or strip-club nights out. Reid was a solid, honest family man. And there was a huge bonus: Veronica. What a lovely, sweet, giving child who would be not only my daughter but Harrison's sister. We would be a happy blended family. I just knew it.

CHAPTER TWELVE

My Angel

Mom's last vestige of normalcy was cooking breakfast for my dad. Mom had never been a morning person, but now that it was her most lucid time of the day she seemed to enjoy making eggs for her husband. Those breakfasts kept her holding on to the real world by a thread. When she stopped doting on George, that was it. Her last connection to a normal life was severed.

My father hired a full-time caregiver for her. She could no longer dress or feed herself. And yet, Mom still managed to give both her caretaker and Dad the slip, and sneak out to find alcohol. The nurse would say, "I turned my back on her for just a second." She was like a hyperactive toddler in her pursuit of wine. Once my mom went to a bar and picked up the news broadcaster John McLaughlin (a resident in the building) and brought him to our apartment as if she had intimate plans! John brought my mother home to safety and obviously was not reciprocating her hazy overtures. John and I became lifelong friends. He and I would have great talks on the beach together about politics and my mission for amputees.

The building in Florida was sort of like a country club. Everybody knew everything. My mother was the building's alcoholic. She stumbled down the stairs, down the street, and went into the bars. Members of their community would help her home, or call the police. More than once, she wound up in the elevators naked. People constantly asked us, "Why don't you *do* something?"

My father, brother, and I had forced her into five or six treatment centers, put her on medications, pursued dozens of sponsors, got her therapy, searched the house daily, hourly, for her stash. We'd begged and bribed her to stop drinking. Nothing took. She would go through the motions, or walk out of treatment and appointments, and start guzzling again as soon as she could get her hands on a bottle. People who judged had no idea how determined this woman was to drink. The final option was to go to court and prove she was a danger to herself. Then we could have put her in an involuntary lockup facility. My father just couldn't do it. He said, "She'll never get out. I won't do that to her."

Doctors told us that even if she stopped drinking immediately, her brain wouldn't recover. The damage was permanent. If she got sober, she would still be delusional. What's more, if she stopped drinking cold turkey, she might have a heart attack like Amy Winehouse. Stopping alcohol abruptly was more physically dangerous than stopping heroin abruptly. Serious alcoholics needed alcohol to physically survive. Every road was a dead end.

What was the lesser of two evils? If we refused to let her drink, Mom sneaked out, ran into traffic, menaced the neighbors, sometimes verbally attacking them, and took the police away from other duties. If Dad gave her alcohol, she'd stay put, but he'd be directly contributing to the disease that turned her brain to mush. Dad made the difficult decision to just give her alcohol. When she left the apartment, she was risking not only her safety but the safety of others. If she drank at home, she was only endangering herself, maybe. He convinced himself that by supplying her with wine, he was protecting her from the fatal heart attack. That was his logic. He gave her cases of wine to keep her in check. Mom would still hide her bottles and drink secretly. The habit was so ingrained that even when it didn't matter anymore, she kept up with the pretense.

We argued about it. I knew he had his reasons, but giving alcohol to an alcoholic seemed like exactly the wrong thing to do. I pushed for involuntary rehab. But I knew that, too, would be awful. Mom was confused, and could barely speak. She didn't always know who we were, or where she was, what she'd done yesterday or last week. Whole days would go by and she'd sit in Dad's office without moving or speaking. She would grind her teeth a lot, very loudly. She sat in the dark, an outline, a shadow of the great beauty and doting mother she used to be. She'd had impeccable style and taste, despite having grown up with nothing. She was always kind and treated every single person she met with great sweetness and dignity in part because she never forgot where she came from. This stunning, elegant, talented, beloved woman was brought down by addiction.

Even in the worst of her dementia, Mom had moments of clarity. During one lucid glimmer, I said, "If you don't go to a treatment center, you're going to die."

She barely glanced at me with blank eyes and said, "Maybe I want to die."

One of the final-stage symptoms of Wernicke-Korsakoff syndrome was apathy. Mom had stopped giving a shit. This was the end of hope. It fell way below rock bottom and there was nothing we could do about it.

*   *   *

"Your mother has a stomachache," said Dad. He called me at home in New York. Reid and I were newly engaged.

"Is it bad?" I asked. She had stomach problems fairly often, from drinking and not eating enough.

"She's been complaining for a couple of days. I don't know. I'll take her to a doctor tomorrow."

Dad hated doctors. If he said he'd take her to one, he had to be really concerned. I was nervous all day, and checked in a few times. No change.

"Your mother passed out on the bed," he said later that night.

"Are you taking her to the doctor tomorrow?" I asked.

"Yeah, I think so."

The next morning, shortly after Mom and Dad woke up, she coughed a couple of times, vomited blood, fell backward on the bed, and took her last two breaths.

"Your mother is dead," Dad said when he called from the apartment. Her body was taken to the morgue by ambulance. We eventually learned the cause of death: an infected septic ulcer in her stomach, yet another common problem for alcoholics.

Dad and I talked about logistics: a funeral, who to tell, etc. I don't remember any of the conversation.

I was alone in my apartment. Harrison was at a play date. I didn't want him to see me upset, so I called his friend's mother and said, "I'm not sure when I can pick up Harrison."

"Okay," she said, suspicious. "Is anything wrong?"

"My mother just died." It was a short conversation. She didn't know what to say to me. I was glad to hang up.

In a daze, I actually kept a meeting at Harrison's school with his preschool teacher. I walked in like a zombie. She asked, "Are you all right?"

"My mother just died."

"I'm so sorry! Was it sudden?" she asked.

How to answer that? It was sudden, in that she coughed up blood and dropped dead. But she'd been on a slow, steady decline for more than seven years.

"It was coming for a while," I said.

"Was she young?"

"Sixty-four."

I tortured myself for quite some time about Dad's not taking Mom to the doctor for that stomachache. She'd been complaining for days, he said. They might've been able to save her life. Dad spent half his life trying to help her. We'd all tried. How could he have known that her stomachache was serious? In her dementia, she'd complain about a headache, and then hallucinate an alien invasion in the next breath. She raved about insects coming out of the walls, and lashed out—verbally and physically—at my father whenever he tried to comfort her. Just getting her to a doctor's office would have been an ordeal.

I called some friends: "My mother died." I repeated it over and over again, hoping that the next time, the numbness would wear off and I'd feel the sorrow I knew was coming. I welcomed it. My mother deserved my grief. Logically, I didn't understand why I was numb from shock over her death. Like I hadn't seen it coming, or imagined it? My mother hadn't been functional for five years. She'd been dependent on a caretaker for three. I'd just hoped that being housebound, she was safe, and that despite the horrible situation, she would hold on for a while. I always hoped and dreamed she would get better.

My Lutheran mom was cremated. (Dad keeps the ashes in a gray marble urn under a picture of her in his house.) We had a funeral in a church right next to the building where we used to live on Central Park West. I spoke about her kindness and beauty, and how brave and loving she was when I had the accident, and all through my life. I remember making pages and pages of notes, but speaking at the podium was a blur. My mom's best friend, Sarah, talked about Ingrid's compassion and generosity and classic elegance. My father and brother were unable to speak publically. Andre's pain was almost unbearable to watch. He was four years younger than me, and only seven when Mom went to rehab for the first time. I wonder if Andre could recall any period of his life when Mom wasn't drunk, in rehab, or struggling to stay sober.

Reid came to the funeral with me, of course. We brought Harrison and Veronica. In fact, Reid paid for my mother's funeral. His father came, too, which I thought was a lovely show of support for his new fiancée. Jonathan, his mother, and his sister also came, as well as Harry and his mother and sister. It was an unlikely gathering of every man I'd been engaged to, and their families. It meant so much to me that all of those people from my past could put aside any ill will to say their good-byes to Ingrid. They all adored her.

Only my dad knew what Ingrid had turned into because of her drinking. He'd been under siege for years. When Mom passed, he felt deep grief and loneliness, but also relief. He'd given her unconditional love, and she hurled back nonsensical cruel obscenities at him, his friends, me, and everyone else she came into contact with. He'd spent the last ten years watching her dignity and mental capacity diminish to nothing. As a result, he turned hard the other way and became a health nut—even more so than during his wheatgrass and yogurt phase. He was obsessed with herbs and vitamins, pouring absurd amounts of money into supplements. He had been devoted to my mother as a caregiver, although they couldn't have had much of a sex life for years.

After her death, George was a free man, and took full advantage. It was embarrassing to witness how he'd chase after much younger women. Even more embarrassing: he caught some of them. Along with his health regimen, the satyriasis was one more way for Dad to feel young and impervious to the horror of a death like Mom's.

Guilt came for me. Did my mother start drinking because of the accident? If I hadn't slipped on the barn cleaner, would she have needed so much wine to dull the pain? She was known to drink before then, before I was born. I'd heard from some of her old friends that Mom was a party girl in her Pan Am days and when she and Dad were dating. My mother's hard-core secret drinking started after my accident. It then returned after the trip to India. She might've turned to wine to get through our rocky adolescent years. Mom wasn't happy to move to Florida, and worried terribly during their financial downturn. It all piled on.

She was emotionally brittle. The changes and challenges other people toughed their way through with sheer will and determination would have been insurmountable for Mom without a glass of wine. Nowadays, someone with her level of anxiety would take Zoloft. But Dad distrusted doctors and medicine. Mom didn't want to make a fuss and was probably born with a predilection to addiction. She self-medicated with Merlot.

"I love to get high," she told me once when I asked why she drank. One was not enough. Five were not enough. Ten. Twenty. A true alcoholic, if she had half a glass, she might as well drink the whole bottle. The whole case.

Months after my mother died, I told Dad about my guilt. "You can't blame the accident," he said. "Your mom had other demons to wrestle with. Things you don't know about."

This was my first clue that my mother may have had a dark streak that could have fueled her drinking. I always accepted my mother for what she was to me—the loving maternal embodiment of sweetness who showered me with attention, who was at my side through highs and lows, and was the only one I could turn to in times of need or tragedy. That was enough. That was everything. I never considered that she may have suffered her own trauma as a child or that there were obstacles she may have needed to overcome. It was not her style to burden her pain. Ever.

She never spoke of her childhood, but I could do the math. I knew Mom was born during World War II. Beyond that, her early life was a mystery to me. It was as if life began when she met my dad. I guess I didn't think it strange that she didn't talk about her formative years. When I was little, my need for her was so great that I was content for her to be my magical angel. Later, she ducked my questions about her childhood, and I didn't press. It wasn't for lack of curiosity. My mother built a wall between her past and me, and I didn't want to acknowledge it, let alone break it. It's as if she couldn't protect herself from her past, but she wanted to protect me.

It's more difficult to explain Dad's silence about it. Although I didn't tell him my feelings until well after Mom's death, it's hard for me to believe he didn't know. What was the big secret anyway? My mother didn't have a dignified death. What could he have been protecting her from? To the contrary, he might have saved me some suffering, as I believed that I was the cause of the unhappiness that led to her alcoholism.

Ingrid's Story (pieced together mostly from Dad)

Her father was drafted to be an SS soldier in the Third Reich. He died in battle when my mother was four. Her earliest memories were of bombs going off, and other horrors. From the age of five, Mom had to rummage on the street for things to eat.

The war widow and her young daughter lived in a one-room apartment in Dortmund, Germany. Mom's mother, my grandmother, got help with their expenses from a string of rowdy boyfriends she brought into their one-bedroom apartment. Mom had to listen to her own mother's degradation night after night. I think losing a limb is easy compared to that. I thought of the scene in the Hitchcock movie *Marnie*. One of the mother's drunk clients went after Marnie, with violent results. That could have been a scene out of my own mother's childhood.

It was, of course, an unimaginably horrible time and many people were forced into desperate acts by the circumstances. Still, it was hard to reconcile the grandmother I remember from my own childhood with this wartime survivor. She visited us in New York a couple of times a year. She was an eccentric woman who couldn't be bothered to speak a word of English. She smoked and had a low, raspy voice. She would look at us and talk really loud, gesturing broadly. We'd sit there and let her go on. My father would glance at me, like, "What the fuck is she talking about?"

Though I have no memory of it, when I was one, my parents took me across the Atlantic on the *QE2*. They dropped me off at Grandma's house in Germany for four weeks so they could travel. I was preverbal when they left, but speaking a quite a bit of German when they came back to get me. My first word was *bitte* (German for "please"). Going from hearing English to German might be why I developed a knack for languages.[1]

As soon as she could, my mother fled to America by boat. She was fourteen, spoke no English, and lived with a distant relative in Connecticut. In exchange for the room, she was expected to clean their house and cook meals like a house servant. Beautiful, young, and lonely, Mom was emotionally and physically vulnerable—the perfect victim for a neighbor who sexually molested her.

She only lasted two years in Connecticut before she ran again. This time, she made it to New York. My mother was discovered and hired by the Perkins Agency to model. (She wasn't tall enough for Ford.) Then she became a Pan Am stewardess. She had lots of boyfriends all over the world—and then came Dad. He was young, funny, smart, and handsome. He didn't tell her he was married with three kids; she didn't let on how damaged she was from her troubled life.

For the first twenty-odd years of Mom's life, she'd gone from one tragic situation to the next. And then, just when she could start to relax in a fairy-tale life as my dad's wife with two healthy kids, bam, the accident. For the worst part of my crisis, she remained sober—or at least highly functional, being there for me 100 percent in every way. As I "got better" and took control of my life, she may have felt it was all right to give up some control of hers, and start (or continue?) drinking.

I didn't want to lose my mother—not to drinking, not to death—but I'm not angry with her. I'm grateful to her and I miss her. What-

---

1   I'm not fluent in five languages as I claimed on the set of *The Real Housewives of New York City*, unless you count "New York" and "Housewife" as languages (I could make a case for it). I speak only three: English, French, and Spanish. My German peaked at age one. I don't know why I made that outrageous claim on the show, but then I don't know why I say a lot of what I say on the show.

ever the reasons for her drinking, it was a disease; I could no more blame her for that than I could blame her if she had been destroyed by cancer rather than wine.

I wish she hadn't kept her past hidden from her family and friends. If she'd opened up and talked about it, her demons might not have controlled her. She'd kept her dark history to herself for so long, it was second nature. She also never wanted to burden her children with the "when I was your age" sad stories. It was not her style. Just like her stash bottles, Mom closely guarded her secrets, to her detriment, until there was nothing left to hide or protect.

Now that I know more of the story, I don't feel guilty about my accident and the toll that must have taken on her. But I do feel an additional loss for not knowing her better during her life. If I had, maybe I could have made a difference. And I can't help but feel some guilt about that.

When I think of you now, Mommy—and I do every day—I think of how you saved *my* life, how you were there for me, how you were my angel. You still are my angel. I love you. Rest in peace. Finally. Rest in peace.

CHAPTER THIRTEEN

My Decade in Court

W‌hen Reid became a single man after seven years of marriage, he was successful, young, and good-looking with one child. Even with his tucked-in T-shirt and phone clipped to his belt, he was a catch. He could have gone the whole "my girlfriend the model" route or just man-whored around for a couple of years. But instead, he sought out an over-thirty almost divorced mother. Clearly, he didn't want to party. He wanted a family. When we got engaged, we talked about having more kids as soon as possible. Biological siblings would be the glue that stuck Harrison and Veronica together. The clock was ticking on my fertility, though. If we were going to have more children, we had to hurry up.

But first, we both had to get divorced.

Soon after my mother's funeral, Harry and I took care of that. After years of back-and-forth, we settled on friendly terms.

Reid's divorce, however, crashed into a wall. And here I thought he wouldn't be able to handle *my* craziness.

When she realized she was definitely going to lose Reid, Jane wanted him back. He was still living at home for legal reasons. She made a heavy-handed attempt to lure him back into her . . . good graces. He rejected her offer flatly, and got even cozier with the couch. After that, Jane seemed obsessed with our relationship.

We were once having breakfast at a coffee shop, and I noticed a woman peering through the windows at us. She just stared at us for ten minutes. "Do you know that woman?" I asked.

"It's Jane," he said. "Just ignore her."

That was the first time I saw her. She was much shorter than me (five three), with brown hair and bangs that covered small, close-set eyes. We were not similar, for sure. She was cute, petite, and sullen. After breakfast, she followed us for a few blocks to my building. When I left later that night, I half expected to find her lurking in the lobby. I felt sorry for her. She'd initiated the split, and now had seller's remorse.

When we next talked, I said to Reid, "For the sake of your family, maybe you should give it another shot with Jane."

"No."

Reid didn't mince words. He'd made his decision, and that was that. By then, he'd learned what had initially inspired her to seek a split. Reid had been the last to know, and he was furious some of his family members knew and hadn't told him. He was done with them, and had zero feelings left for his ex.

Jane finally understood that Reid and I were engaged and not breaking up, no matter how hard she glared. So she gave up trying to get him back, and then swung *hard* in the other direction. She filed papers with the court calling me a "paramour," and seeking a ban on play dates between Harrison and Veronica. That didn't pan out.

Her next gambit was to wake up a sleeping Reid and start screaming at him. He had done some organizing and cleaning while she was away for the weekend. She flipped out over his touching her stuff. Reid refused to engage, and locked himself in another room. In a fury, Jane called the police. When they arrived, the lead officer asked, "We got a call about a domestic disturbance. What's going on?"

Reid said, "I cleaned the apartment."

She said, "He pushed me!"

That was it. Any allegation of abuse had to be investigated. Jane accused him of shoving her around while Veronica was sleeping in the next room. Reid called me the next morning and said, "You won't believe what happened." I was in shock.

There was another incident a few days later. Jane became aggressive with Reid. What Jane forgot: the nanny cam in the living room of their apartment was on and recording. It taped both incidents, from her waking him up, pulling his covers off of him, screaming at him, his leaving the room and closing the door, right to the police arriving. It was all on camera.

Reid brought the tape to the police station and showed them the video. They were not happy to see it. Officers don't like to be lied to, especially about domestic violence. It was a serious crime. False accusations make it harder for real victims. While Reid took Veronica to get ice cream, the police went to Jane's office to arrest her.

Reid came to my place and told me what was going on. I was horrified. "Are you sure about this?" I asked. "You want to arrest the *mother of your child?*"

He looked me dead in the eye, and said, "Yes."

While Jane cooled her heels in lockup, the district attorney sat down with Reid and explained what would happen next. "If you press charges, your wife could face prison time," he said.

Reid nodded. "I'll bring our daughter to visit her there," he said.

Whoa. This was the moment I realized nice, normal Reid turned into a stone-cold assassin when crossed. He didn't seek out trouble. He let wrong come to him. And when it did, he'd wait for his opening, and then he attacked. His enemy had no idea what hit him (or her). I had to admit: it was a turn-on.

Jane spent the night in jail. If it were me, I would have broken after ten minutes behind bars and started crying and begging for forgiveness. But she came out cool and collected, like she was leaving a ladies' tea. This was one tough cookie.

On Valentine's Day 2005, the warring parties had an emergency court hearing about the false accusation charge. Reid's lawyer, Sue Moss, wheeled a video player on a dolly into the courtroom and said, "I have the evidence right here that proves what really happened that day."

The judge said, "Stop right there. I suggest you all go outside and settle this right now."

He didn't mean the false accusation. He meant the entire divorce. They'd been fighting over money, property, and custody for a year. This false accusation was proof that they were spiraling downhill, and it could only get worse. The judge ordered them to end it right now and move on with their lives.

From the beginning, Jane wanted fifty-fifty custody, a fifty-fifty split of the apartment, a fifty-fifty split of their property. She had a job, and they'd always had an equal marriage when it came to chores and responsibilities. Jane was big on that—even wanting Reid to clean exactly half of the dishes. (Call me crazy, but I always thought that being uncalculating and giving more was a secret to a great marriage or divorce.) After he and I started dating, though, she upped her demands, insisting on more money and full custody.

As the judge advised, Reid and Jane and their lawyers went into the hallway and brokered a new deal. She agreed to Reid's generous child support payment and fifty-fifty custody of Veronica. She would spend one week with her mom, and then one week with her dad. They returned to the courtroom. The judge approved the settlement. "Now, about this apartment," he said. "Living together is not a good idea. Until the apartment is sold, Veronica will stay in the apartment and you will each move out for half the week." Reid was all too happy to agree to that. They would still share the place, but not have to be there together.

Thanks to the nanny cam, Reid had the leverage he needed. If not for that tape, the divorce would have dragged on for years to come, no doubt getting uglier and uglier along the way.

They signed the papers. Reid was elated. He called that Valentine's Day one of the greatest days of his life. Jane moved out for her off part of the week and I went to Reid's apartment for the first time. Jane knew I'd be there. Just to make sure I didn't touch her stuff (she was very sensitive about that), she labeled her food in the fridge. I was warned by their baby-sitter not to eat these little mini boxes of cereal (the kind you get at a hotel) in the pantry. "Oh, no!" she said. "You can't have that! It's Jane's!"

She had a set of china from Versace. For whatever reason, Jane decided that if I came to the apartment, I would steal her china. I am not a thief and the china wasn't to my taste at all. (Have you *seen*

Versace china?) Apparently, she'd railed at Reid for an hour, "Aviva better not steal my china!" Reid relayed the message to me. I was dumbfounded and cracked up. Did she think I'd tuck a dessert plate into my purse and slink away into the night? It was just such a bizarre thing to fixate on.

Then again, who was I to talk about fixating on bizarre things?

I figured in her view, I'd already stolen something far more precious to her than a sugar bowl. The woman was in pain, and lashed out in any way she could. She didn't let up even after their divorce was final.

When their apartment finally sold, Reid took a three-bedroom in the same building as mine on Sixty-first Street and York. His apartment was directly above mine. It would have been too abrupt to move in together right away. Veronica and Harrison needed a transition period before we could be a full-time family. We might as well have been, though. We were constantly going up and down the stairs between 7B and 8B. When Reid had custody of Veronica, we ate together at his place. When she was with her mother, Reid basically lived at my apartment. That summer, we rented a house in the Hamptons. The kids had birthday parties out there, and we really felt like a family. We were madly in love. The kids grew accustomed to being a four-person unit. Compared to the summer before in Miami with my parents, this was bliss.

The only chink in our happiness continued to be Jane. She was so angry and resentful. When I picked up Veronica for our custody days, Jane narrowed those malevolent eyes at me, like she wanted to turn me to stone. Reid nicknamed her Medusa. You'd think Jane would have been relieved that he chose a mother and not some inexperienced twenty-five-year-old floozie. Oh, well. She was hurt and angry, and all the smiles and kindness in the world were not going to change that.

Friends have told me that when a stepmother tried to be like a second mother, the birth mom could get territorial and competitive. Jane pushed back over anything I did for Veronica. She didn't like the clothes I bought for her. The dresses and tops were too fancy and European. She preferred her daughter to dress in casual T-shirts from Old Navy. I bathed Veronica, helped potty train her, and cooked for her and shopped with her. I treated her no differently than Harrison, and did everything possible to make her feel comfortable and happy. I loved her like my own. Jane tried to undermine my relationship with Veronica. I felt like I could do no right. It was a lose-lose situation. Being a stepmom with an unsupportive bio mom seemed impossible.

And then I got pregnant. The minute Reid and I were both divorced, we started trying to have a baby. I figured it would take awhile to get pregnant in my mid-thirties. But it happened on our first shot. Reid wanted to get married ASAP.

My first wedding was supposed to be huge. The second was medium sized. My third wedding would be small. Really small. Even "just family" felt too crowded by then. Our extended families were growing smaller all the time, by death and by choice. Mom had died. Reid was barely on speaking terms with his father and stepmother.

I'd only met his father and stepmom a few times over dinner. They seemed to appreciate my efforts to care for and love Veronica. They adored Harrison and were very loving toward him. They clearly got that Reid and I were deeply in love. However, they were way too cozy with Jane for Reid's taste during a very difficult time. Reid and Jane were always at war over one thing or another. His father and stepmother's continued relationship with her felt like a huge betrayal.

We sat down with them to talk about it. Reid said, "Blood is thicker than water. Jane is causing us nothing but grief. She lied and tried to have me arrested. She is constantly trying to hurt my new family. Why on earth are you spending so much time with her?"

"We want to see our granddaughter," said Mr. Drescher.

"But we have fifty-fifty custody and live four blocks away from you," said Reid. "You can see Veronica whenever you want."

But their visits with Jane continued. Through and by their actions, they were being very unsupportive of Reid and his new family unit. I felt they were being disrespectful to me. It. Made. No. Sense. The most complicated part of it all was that Reid's father was Chief Financial Officer of Reid's firm, Spencer Clarke.

By the time of our wedding, relations with them were too strained. They weren't acting like family, so Reid didn't want to include them in the plans. My father hated weddings. He thought they were a waste of money and stupid and wouldn't come. We made a few tentative lists of people to invite, and ultimately decided that it was all too complicated and tricky. In the end, we made it super simple. Reid and me, and Harrison and Veronica. Our family. The reason we were getting married.

The ceremony was at the Brotherhood Synagogue overlooking Gramercy Park. My half sister's husband, a rabbi, ran the place. He officiated the service. I wore a raw silk button-down ivory dress with three-quarter-length sleeves and a collar, a belt, and a full skirt. It was appropriate, I thought, for the second wedding of a newly pregnant, middle-aged bride. The kids were dressed up and looked adorable. As they walked down the aisle, they threw rose petals. I felt blessed to have our three children there, including Hudson, who was in my belly. After the service, we went to Gramercy Park to take pictures, and then to the Regency Hotel for lunch.

It was a beautiful low-key day for just us. I could have gone on the way we were and had Hudson (formerly known as Brandon—nutcase me, I changed his name when he was four months old) out of wedlock. After what we'd both been through in our divorces, it seemed insane to rush right into another marriage. But Reid really wanted that piece of paper. He felt like it was the right thing to do for the children to have legally married parents.

Our newlywed year, I took my job as a stepmother very seriously. I tried to walk that edge of treating Veronica like my own child without stepping on Jane's toes. I went all out to make peace with her for Veronica's sake. For long stretches, we were civil. There were times when we chatted on the phone like girlfriends. I made it clear that Veronica was her daughter. I had no intention of doing anything she didn't approve of. At the end of the day, no matter how hard I tried, I just could not get it right.

We had 50 percent custody of Veronica. During that time, I picked up Veronica at school. I took her to her activities. I played and read with her, took her to art class, arranged play dates and birthday parties, and really enjoyed shopping for her. I loved putting her hair in bows to match the smock dresses. Whatever she needed, I took care of it. But the more I loved Veronica, and the more she loved me, the more strained Jane and I became. Our friendly phone calls turned surly and rude.

As I approached my due date with Hudson, Reid's father and stepmother were still in an unholy alliance with his ex. Reid asked Jane flat out to give his family some space. An impartial mediator got involved, and he agreed that Jane's clinging to Reid's family was not healthy. She apologized for causing tension and promised to back off. But a week later, she dropped by their place again. Reid's father and stepmother never understood how betrayed we felt.

She seemed to have ulterior motives. The next thing you know, we were back to court. This cycle repeated itself for four years. After the third lawsuit with an affidavit that included comments about her relationship with his father and stepmom, Reid had had enough. He fired his father. The stone-cold assassin came out. Do not fuck with Reid. He looked like a nerdy nice guy, but when you pushed him too far, he was lethal.

Several years have passed since then. These strained relationships are improving. For the children's sake, we are forging forward, trying to mend what has been broken, and hope to have harmony in the family that extends beyond our unit of six.

In 2008, eight months after Hudson was born, I decided to celebrate the end of nursing by taking a bath. It may not sound like much of a celebration, but it was like a weekend in the Bahamas for me. With two older kids and a new baby, I'd been too busy to carve out half an hour for myself. The tub in our apartment had Jacuzzi jets and I'd fantasized about taking a bath in it for months. I filled it up, turned on the whirl, and soaked in the bubbles for a delicious hour.

One week later, I came down with a sudden high temperature. This quickly turned into full-blown sickness with night sweats, fever, coughing. It was so bad, I asked my doctor, Dr. Kruger, to meet me at his office on a Saturday. I looked gray. He said, "It's a virus," and put me on antibiotics.

Two days later I felt even worse. The night sweats were so bad I had to change the sheets a few times each night. I was so sick that my mother-in-law had to spoon-feed me. I went back to Dr. Kruger's office. I must have looked like shit, because he sent me for a chest

X-ray. After the radiologist called him, he brought me right back into his office.

"Have you been traveling overseas?" he asked. "Staying in any hotels?"

I'd been trapped in my apartment with the baby. "Uh, no," I said.

He put up my X-rays on the light box. "You've got severe pneumonia in both lungs."

Hospitalization Number . . . What? Fifteen?

I didn't spend very long in the hospital. Dr. Kruger drew blood, put me on powerful antibiotics, and kept me under observation.

I was released after a day. Two days later, I went to Dr. Kruger's office *again*. He had the results of my blood test.

"Aviva," he said, "I have some bad news and good news."

"Tell me," I said.

"The bad news is that you have Legionnaires' disease. The good news is that the antibiotics I gave you for the pneumonia are exactly the right course to treat Legionnaires'."

Legionnaires' disease? The thing you catch on cruise ships? I did some Googling. It was first discovered in 1976 at an American Legion convention at the Bellevue-Stratford hotel in Philadelphia. Apparently, this potentially fatal disease (if not caught early, mortality rates are as high as 50 percent) is caused by bacteria that lives in water tanks and is spread via air-conditioning, humidifiers, fountains, ice machines, any such system that can turn infected water into a mist. How the hell did I catch it in my own home? Were my kids susceptible? I freaked out, of course, and hired a scientific investigator.

It was the damn Jacuzzi. Bacteria was in the pipes and when the bubbles turned the hot water into steam, I inhaled it. You see why I'm a hypochondriac? Because if anyone is going to get a hotel disease in her own bathroom, it's me. Dr. Kruger was an absolutely brilliant diagnostician to think of testing me for Legionnaires'. He had no reason to do so; it's that rare. Well, I survived it. But I never took a bath in that tub again. Hot tubs used to be a great pleasure, but now I look at them and think instantly of my mother-in-law feeding me with a spoon. (Forgot to add Jacuzzis to my list of phobias. . . .)

Meanwhile, my happy settlement with Harry turned decidedly unfriendly. As soon as Reid and I got married, Harry didn't have to pay alimony. But he was still obliged to pay child support for Harrison. In 2009, the checks more or less stopped coming. Reid took on all of Harrison's expenses, in addition to his own monthly child support he paid to Jane. It was the start of the recession, and everyone felt the squeeze. Reid wanted me to press Harry to come up with what he owed. I begged Harry to make good on his child support. The check was always "in the mail."

I waited six months, and then I took Harry to court. Harry claimed poverty. My lawyer Sue Moss's due diligence proved that Harry still charged a large monthly amount for himself. He was going out every night, flying around, living part time in Los Angeles. If he had ample funds to party till dawn, then he could dole out a bit of child support. I wasn't looking for anything beyond what he was legally obligated to pay. At one point, Reid questioned whether we should pursue the lawsuit. But I was adamant. It was the principle of it all. Harrison deserved what was rightfully his.

While not paying his child support, Harry dated LuAnn de Lesseps for a hot minute. It was LuAnn's single year, after her divorce from the Count but before she met her now-fiancé Jacques. I knew LuAnn. We had a mutual friend. I remember telling our friend that it wouldn't look good for LuAnn to date Harry on her TV show. His scenes with her didn't air, fortunately for LuAnn. He did appear in a scene on *Real Housewives* season four, spanking his old friend Sonja Morgan's butt at the costume party when she forgot to wear panties under her costume. He wasn't exactly hiding his head in shame.

For over four years, Harry missed most of his monthly payments. I was in and out of court throughout that time, pleading with the judge for help. Finally, he put the gavel down and gave Harry thirty days to come up with a large sum or go to jail. Harry had been crying poor for four years. But as soon as the judge said "jail," a check arrived the next day for the full amount. It was only a fraction of what he owed, but I would take what I could get.

That was the last monthly payment I received. His family was sick to death of me after three years of divorce court and four years of family court. I bet they were also sick of Harry. They offered me a lump sum of child support for Harrison that was supposed to last until his emancipation at age twenty-one. Basically, they were going to pay me to go away. The amount was much lower than what I was already legally owed. They wanted to cut the settlement amount by less than half. The Dubins were extraordinarily wealthy people. They could easily afford to honor Harry's child support obligations. I never understood why everyone expected Reid to pick up the tab.

Harrison was their only grandson, the only one who would take their name. He was a bright, handsome, funny, polite, big-hearted child. I honestly had no idea why they acted this way. I am sure it was not personal against Harrison. Sometimes anger clouds people's actions. It seems as though Harrison's best interests got lost temporarily by his grandparents.

The situation was so dysfunctional that taking the lump sum, even at a huge loss, might be the wisest decision. I had a family to think about. Reid and I were exhausted from this battle. We decided that life was too short to spend another day in court. It was enough money to ensure part of my son's future. But still, t wasn't so easy to walk away.

The one thing the Dubins *were* paying all along was Harrison's tuition. In May 2012, right before my first season of *The Real Housewives of New York City* was to air, Harrison's school called. The finance person said, "Your ex-husband signed the school contract last year, but he hasn't paid a penny. You have to pay last year's tuition and next year's tuition in full if you want to keep Harrison in school." Harry, of course, hadn't told me that the tuition wasn't paid.

We owed the school around eighty thousand dollars. I didn't want to ask Reid for more money. He had already been footing the bill for years. I thought about sending Harrison to public school. But our other kids were in private; it felt wrong. Reid kept telling me that he would take care of it. I waited to see if the Dubins would cough up the tuition, as they always did for all their grandchildren. Letters between lawyers flew like grenades. Somehow or other, my battles with Harry got picked up by the *New York Post*, which ran two separate articles about them over the summer.

And then my season on *Real Housewives* started airing. Sonja Morgan knew I'd been married to Harry, and she went on and on about what a great guy he was, how much fun, what a great lover, and so on. Everyone was wild about Harry, as long as they didn't depend on him for child support! I sat there, and listened to it all, agreeing and smiling.

"Oh, yes. Harry is just awesome," I said and smiled, biting my cheek, during filming.

I never complained about the pressure he put on me and my family, or the lawsuits, or the unpaid bills. I never bad-mouthed Harry on camera. I simply would not wave my dirty laundry about my son's father on national TV. Before I shot my first scene, I drew that line. No matter what anyone said about Harry, I would smile and nod. That was the deal I made with myself, and I kept it. Off camera, I told the girls the truth and stuff leaked to the press.

I wavered about taking the lump sum, or fighting to uphold the settlement we already had. The critical moment came in the winter of 2013. Harrison Googled himself and found those *New York Post* articles. He had no idea that any of this had been going on *for years*. Reid, Harry, and I had shielded him from the legal issues completely. When he found out, he got very upset. I'd become a public person. I realized I had to change my tactics. To fight for my son after being on a national television show, I had to keep our private business out of the press.

I took the lump sum. As soon as I decided to take it, I felt lighter and happier. Harry will always be a part of our lives, but given his behavior, it's hard to be a full member of the Harry-is-a-Great-Guy fan club. Harry has a kind nature, but his weaknesses hurt others. They've hurt us. I have chosen to overlook it for the greater good.

❋　❋　❋

On another front, Jane dropped another legal bomb on us, too! It all started over a disagreement about whether or not Veronica should take fish oil supplements. I was obsessed with vitamins, and gave fish oil to all my children. (What? *Vitamins for children? Insane!*) Among other things, Jane was against it. When she objected, I stopped giving Veronica the pills. But Jane had to make a federal case about it, and used it as a starting point for another lawsuit.

Only a week after Jane gave birth to her second baby with her second husband, her lawyers delivered a hundred-page lawsuit to us. She was suing Reid for full custody of Veronica and, of course, *more money*. This odious document was punctuated by vicious lies. She produced every single email we'd ever exchanged—hundreds of earth-shattering gems like, "Veronica has a play date today with Samantha. Okay?"—as examples of my being an "overinvolved step-mother." My active stepparenting of Veronica, she claimed, made it impossible for her to coparent with Reid.

There were fifty pages about how "overinvolved" I was in Veronica's life, listing all the things I did for the girl, like take her to doctor's appointments, help her with homework, make her food, buy her nice clothes, throw her birthday parties, and other horrible abuses of power.

Reid and I read the pages. They cited emails and examples dating from when Veronica was a baby. "She's been plotting this lawsuit *for years*," I said. "Why file it now?"

"She wants to move to Long Island with her husband and babies," Reid explained. She had already moved to Queens, causing Veronica a longer commute to school. The longer distance would mean a huge disruption in Veronica's routine—and Jane's. If she had full custody, she wouldn't have to schlepp her daughter to school and our place and back. In the original agreement, both parties agreed to stay in Manhattan.

Reid was livid. I'd never seen him as angry as he was when we had to go to court, *again,* over this ridiculous fiction. She should have peddled it in Hollywood. She would have had a better reception than in Manhattan family court.

By luck of the draw, the judge was the same man who handled my child support case with Harry. When he saw Reid walk into the courtroom, he said, "You, again?" Quickly, he pieced the whole saga together. He already knew Reid supported Harrison during Harry's delinquent years. He knew that we had other children as well, and that Reid was a stand-up guy.

The judge listened to the arguments. He read Jane's papers, and our defense. Then he called Reid and Jane back to court for his decision. He said, "I have people walking in and out of this room every day. I have never seen anyone bend over backward to try to keep things as amicable as the Dreschers. Jane, you should consider yourself *lucky* that Veronica's stepmother is involved and cares and keeps the lines of communication open between you. You know what? You folks co-parent better than 95 percent of the people who come through my courtroom. This case seems like a lot of nonsense and I don't appreciate the lying. This case is not for court. Dismissed."

The judge openly called her a liar in court.

Her case was thrown out.

Reid was pissed off over this entire fiasco and ready to go into assassin mode. He would not speak to Jane directly, and hadn't for the two years since this last lawsuit. The court assigned them a mediator. *To this day,* they have monthly meetings with the mediator to discuss Veronica. Brilliant or absurd? A little of both. On the bright side, they have not been in court since, but it is a bit odd to continue seeing your ex-spouse monthly in a therapist's office. If you wanted to fight in an expensive counselor's office with a man, you might as well be married to him! Of course, it was healthy to check in about coparenting your child. They both love Veronica and want the best for her. But her insisting on monthly sessions? To me, that seems like holding on to the past. I think it would be healthier for Jane to let go of Reid. However, I could understand how it would be hard to get over him. I can understand her still hanging on. I am not sure how her husband feels about it though.

Although we won, I felt defeated. I'd lost years in court. None of those battles should have been waged. Now that it was over, the weight of what we'd been through hit me full force. I'd fought for my son, and been blasted. As a stepmother, I tried to be as close and involved as a real mom, and we got sued for it. At the peak of frustration, I thought I should back off from Veronica so Jane wouldn't snap. But I'd known Veronica since she was a baby. I loved this bright, sweet, beautiful child. How *could* I back off emotionally? Well, I couldn't.

How to deal with irrational people? How to absorb their terrible behavior? Over the years, Jane systematically tried to destroy Reid's sacred relationships. A son and his father. A father and his daughter. A husband and his wife. The real victim in all of this was Veronica, of course. The girl could have two sets of loving parents who worked in concert to raise a happy, healthy child. But that would be a perfect world.

In the real world, we've had to walk on eggshells, which wasn't so easy for me to do. I should add lawsuits to my list of anxieties and phobias. I did live in fear of the next crisis. If Veronica and Harrison had a minor sibling spat, like in every family, I worried that Veronica would run to her mom about it. Jane would freak out and demand hours of mediation. In all these years, Jane has gained nothing except huge legal bills and a daughter who knows the two homes are not at all in sync. But those facts never stopped her.

CHAPTER FOURTEEN

Our Modern Family

As parents, our destiny seems to be to screw up the kids, to pass neuroses onto our own kids. You know all about my neuroses, but I still came out okay. And my brother Andre came out fantastic. He's a great uncle—amazing with children—and a really excellent guy. I think he looks like Marky Mark and he has a kind and protective personality. He has a cool job with a WiFi company in Miami and is not a party boy or a model chaser *and* he is single. Ladies, grab him! He is one of the last few great ones out there! He has always been there for me, even when we were children. When I was scared at night, I would hobble over to his room and pull out the trundle to sleep near him. (Okay, that was every night.) As we got older he loved the men in my life who were good to me and wanted to kill those who were not. A smart man, he refused to go on *Real Housewives* last season.

Meanwhile, I'm probably screwing up my kids in ways I can and can't imagine.

Fade in:

Interior: Therapist's Office—Day
It's the year 2043. Thirty-two-year-old Sienna
is on the couch.

SIENNA: . . . and then my mother went on *Real Housewives of New York City!*
THERAPIST: Oh my god! You poor kid!
SIENNA: Yes, I know.
THERAPIST: Hey, did you ever meet Ramona? She was always my favorite.

In Oscar Wilde's play *A Woman of No Importance* (which would have been the title of this book if it hadn't already been taken), Lord Illingworth tells Mrs. Arbuthnot, "Children begin by loving their parents. After a time they judge them. Rarely, if ever, do they forgive them." For my own, I hope they won't judge me too harshly, and will eventually, with years of therapy, forgive me. Until then, I'm trying to immerse them in normalcy and continue blocking them from watching Bravo.

I don't believe I have so much to do with my children's outcomes. They come out the way they come out. I can encourage their strengths and try to improve their weaknesses. I teach them to be curious, kind, and polite, and to celebrate differences. Besides that, I do my best to raise them to be good people and the rest is up to them.

As someone who grew up in a dysfunctional family (really, is there any other kind?), my refuge is in the commonplace. As my dad's eccentricities became ever more odd (Sai Baba, anyone?) and my mom's warmth disintegrated into alcoholic despair, I was nostalgic for the comfort of tedium. I was happiest growing up when I felt average. I'm glad to report that our modern blended family is painfully normal and boring. Or so I think. I might be wrong. We did have some not-so-boring moments, from the kids' very inceptions . . .

I was in misery every minute of my three pregnancies. It was like my body had been invaded by a foreign enemy. Because of my drug phobia, I couldn't take Advil for a headache or Pepto-Bismol for a stomachache. I just gritted my teeth and got through it. The only part I truly loved was the kicking and squirming, feeling the life inside of me. That was so incredible, it mitigated the nausea a little.

Being a monoped was an added pregnancy complication. When the center of my gravity changed, it threw off my balance with my prosthesis. I had to readjust my gait. Also, weight gain made it harder to put on the prosthesis. Compared to pregnancy though, labor and delivery were easy peasy for me—the first two, anyway. My threshold for pain might be higher than most. I found birthing to be a civilized process. I had an epidural, waited to dilate, and then pushed my babies out in five minutes. I could have shot them across the room (strong muscles). During my first birth with Harrison, I took the prosthesis off. With Hudson and Sienna, I kept it on. My doctor suggested it, because it was easier to keep myself in the stirrups and bear down.

Reid does not faint at the sight of blood. He was an active participant in the births of Hudson and Sienna. He would have snapped on gloves and taken over for the doctor if need be. I'm not fond of squeamish people. We are all made up of blood and guts. We all poop and pee and other gross stuff. Reid proved himself to be unafraid of gore and gunk during my labors. He was there for me, in the room and at my side. The type of guy you want to marry, in my opinion, is the one who can watch the baby come out of the vagina and still want to go back there. A real man, like Reid, can deal with it.

After two boys, I really wanted a girl, and so did Reid. We did some research. Gender of the baby was determined by the sperm, which supplied either an X or a Y chromosome. The mother's egg always contained an X chromosome. It was possible to separate the X from the Y sperm, and implant the chosen flavor, as it were, into the uterus during ovulation. So we started looking for a doctor who would "spin sperm." It wasn't an expensive procedure, only a thousand dollars. It might seem weird sciencey, but if I could tip the odds in favor of a girl, I was willing to try.

At the time, my friend's mother was dying of cancer in Palm Beach. I was up all night thinking about her one night, and unable to sleep. Reid couldn't sleep with my tossing and turning. So what did we do wide awake at 3 a.m.?

I got pregnant that night. No sperm spinning for us. When we found out, I looked at Reid and jokingly said, "If this is a boy, I am going to kill you." Boy or girl, at thirty-nine, I knew it was my last pregnancy. At the seventeen-week sonogram, we learned we were having a girl. And Reid's life was saved.

It was the end of summer 2010. Reid and I were watching *Californication* in bed. Sienna (we had the name picked out already) was going crazy inside me. I turned to Reid and said, "She's kicking like a black belt. I'm surprised my water isn't—"

Pop. I felt the trickle. I clicked on my leg and ran to the bathroom. Yup, my water broke. I called our doctor. He said, "Stay put and wait a few hours for the contractions to get closer together. If anything else happens, go to the hospital."

Like I needed the invitation? "Got it," I said. My previous labors took six or seven hours. With Hudson, I had to be induced. So I figured I had plenty of time at home. We settled in, assuming we'd have at least until four or five in the morning.

Half an hour later, my contractions came on strong, like nothing I'd felt before with either of my sons. I called the doctor back. "We're going in," I said.

Reid and I raced to New York–Presbyterian hospital in a cab. I was writhing in pain and gulping for air in the backseat. When we arrived at the prebirthing triage area, I was in agony. It was happening way too fast. I started worrying that something was wrong. I got in a birthing room by 1 a.m. A nurse examined me. "You're fully dilated," she said.

I was already in full labor, an hour after my first cramp.

The anesthesiologist came in with his cart.

"Are you ready for an epidural?" he asked.

"Yes! But you can't give me Fentanyl. I'm allergic to it." I wasn't really allergic. But I hated that drug. It is a derivative of morphine. I had it during my labor with Hudson, and felt that horrible floating sensation I've feared since I was six.

We went back and forth about it. The anesthesiologist complained he'd have to go to the hospital pharmacy to get something else.

"So do it!" I yelled. He was giving me a hard time when I was in full labor? I might've been a little rude to him. But finally, he got it in his head that I knew what I was talking about, and prepared another needle.

Five minutes after getting my epidural, the doctor walked in and said, "Okay, Aviva. Time to deliver."

"The epidural hasn't kicked in yet," I said.

He frowned at me. "You're crowning. You have to start pushing now. You can do it. If anyone can do this, it's you."

"I don't know if I can," I said.

I did. During my first two births, I was numb. That was why pushing was so easy. This time, I felt the whole thing. It was like shitting out a television set. Fortunately, it happened really fast. Sienna was born by 4 a.m. She practically skipped down my leg at birth. We brought our baby girl home the next day, and our family was complete. Two boys, two girls. At the time of this writing, Harrison is eleven, Veronica, ten, Hudson, five, and Sienna is still my baby at two.

I breast-fed each baby for about a year. I made so much milk, I could have sold some of it and had bottles to spare. I only stopped with Hudson when he had enough teeth to bite my nipple. Sienna still gets some breast milk. I was recently stopped at the airport with a cooler of it. When the TSA says no more than four ounces of *any* liquid, they mean it.

The kids are all so different, which never ceases to amaze me. Harrison is built like a football player, but he's gentle at heart, charismatic and social. Veronica is sweet-natured and so smart. She's an avid reader and is already much smarter than me. Hudson is a replica of Reid. If you know Reid, you know Hudson. He's already trying to work around the house and do chores for money. Sienna is my baby, but she won't be last fiddle. She seems to have been put on this earth to just love all day long.

They all eat differently. Every night our home is like a restaurant and every child gets a different meal according to his or her needs. (I am such a sucker.) The other night, Veronica said, "You know, the food here is like gourmet food."

I said, "Oh, my God! Thank you!"

Then Harrison chimed in, "It's not a compliment, Mom. Kids *hate* gourmet food."

On any given night, I will make a salad and piece of grilled chicken for Harrison, who has a big appetite and can only fill up if he eats a lot of veggies. For Veronica, who is super skinny and picky, I stir-fry some shrimp and carrots. Every night, I boil pasta for her, in case she refuses to eat the other options. Hudson was diagnosed with a feeding disorder and a failure to thrive as a baby. At age one, he couldn't eat solid food and was severely underweight. A therapist had to come to the house five times per week to exercise his oral motor muscles. We managed to get enough calories in him without a feeding tube. But he still struggles, and only eats a few types of food: ravioli, pizza, chicken fingers, fries, and meatballs. He has never tasted a fruit or a vegetable in his life. He won't put them in his mouth. Sienna is the only kid who will eat anything. For my husband, I do my best to keep our dinners healthy and fun. The meat is grass fed, the chicken free range and organic. I use plenty of anti-inflammatory, anticancer turmeric and cumin. Our fruits and vegetables are pesticide free. I serve antioxidant-rich blueberries, raspberries, and strawberries for dessert. It's a bit of a buzz kill.

I cook with stainless steel only. None of my cookware has Teflon or nonstick surfaces. I avoid aluminum foil. I am a supporter of Trash Cancer, Fran Drescher's charity that educates people on how to lower the level of carcinogens in their home. I know it all sounds very obsessive and overprotective. Look, anyone can get hit by a truck or get cancer. You never know what's going to happen. But, in my opinion, you can stack the odds in your favor by avoiding pesticides and chemicals in the food you eat.

I realize I've picked up a little of my father's obsessiveness about food. But the only fad I follow is whole, organic, healthy. Like Dad, I take vitamins, including D and C, a multi, and fish oil supplements. We all do (except Veronica). I do loosen up and put out junk food for special occasions. If we have a Super Bowl party, I will serve Doritos, even soda. (Not Coke, though. That stuff puts me over the edge.) We will do sliders and pigs in a blanket, although I think hot dogs are toxic. Nitrates are the worst.

They're just four fairly normal kids in a fairly normal family. Now you know my secret: I *really* am a real housewife and real mother, not a reality character. How boring!

CHAPTER FIFTEEN

Housewives

In season five of *The Real Housewives of New York City*, shortly after arriving in Saint Bart's, I got into a screaming match with Ramona and Sonja and called them both "white trash." White trash? Really, Aviva? God, who is that bitch, that shrieking banshee? I know one thing. It's not me. It couldn't be. I don't speak to people like that. I'm a good person, devoted to family and public service. I try to be sensitive, tolerant, kind, generous, and loving. Did I really just call those women "white trash"? It couldn't be me.

All right, it *was* me. Well, not *me*, per se, but me in an altered state. I did argue; I did fight; and I did call them by that vile phrase. How do these things happen? I was trying to preserve my dignity, and oopsy—I blew it. For myself at least.

I could give you a number of lame excuses—excuses that are true, mind you, but excuses nonetheless. And frankly, there really isn't any excuse for my behavior. I'm ashamed of myself. I apologized and tried to make things right on the reunion show in hopes that Ramona and Sonja could forgive me. The good news is that I was brought back for another season of *Housewives*.

I get a vibe from some people that they think I believe that I'm in some way better than them, that I'm a snob. Maybe I am a bit of a snob. The thing is, it's not that I think I'm better than they are, it's just that I like *my* taste more than I like *theirs*. It's just human nature. I prefer my Kraft Macaroni and Cheese to your, say, Stouffer's Macaroni and Cheese. I'm not judging your goddamn white-trash macaroni and cheese. I just like mine better. I don't think that makes me a snob. I try not to make a show of my taste. But I tend toward the classic styles in literature, music, dress, and art. Those of us who do will always be accused of snobbery. Still, there's nothing elegant about saying what I said. I felt attacked. And I'm not pretty when I'm attacked. I surprised and shocked myself when that über-cranky bitch came out. I am usually pretty unruffled—unless you screw with my family. Then the mama bear comes out. So I'm copping to it: that nutty lady is a small part of me. A footnote, I hope, and I want you to have the full story. That's why I wrote this book.

I know a lot of readers probably skipped right to this chapter to get the "dirt" on *The Real Housewives*. And believe me I understand. I probably would have done the same thing. But before going on, I'd love it if you went back to the beginning and read about my life up to this point. My turning into a Real Housewife is much more interesting if you know how I got there.

And, oh, by the way, there really isn't any dirt. One thing about *The Real Housewives* . . . it's all up there on the screen.

I watched *The Real Housewives of New York City* sporadically during its first several seasons. I didn't think I related to it much, but it was well done, the women seemed interesting, and what the hell—I watch TV for escape. One night, I turned it on in bed with Reid. He was horrified.

"I'm never watching this again," he said. "It's banned." I didn't argue. I'm going to get into a fight over a stupid reality show? *Please.* Men don't get the appeal. Reid found it unendurable. I didn't blame him for loathing the show. On the other hand, I can't stand *Dexter*, one of Reid's favorites, in which the hero is a serial killer. Reid insists it's less violent than *Real Housewives.*

Even though the show didn't hold any particular meaning for me, I did get a kick out of watching LuAnn de Lesseps. We'd met before at a party at our mutual friend Maria's house. LuAnn was standing next to me, and I said, "You are so stunning."

She laughed and said, "So are you!" Ha! I was pregnant with Hudson and was enormous. But I accepted the compliment. Isn't that just so *Housewives?* Two women gushing about how fabulous they look at a party? Anyway, Reid and LuAnn's husband the Count started talking. (I had no idea anyone was a Count or Countess. I did not even know what that was until the show introduced LuAnn.) The four of us had dinner one night and we tried to get together again, but it just didn't pan out. A year later, the first season of the show aired, and I was pleasantly surprised to see her on it. I was all, *Go, LuAnn!* I thought that was the closest connection I'd ever have with the show.

In the summer of 2010, my childhood friend Jake told me that Bravo was searching for a new housewife for the show. He'd described me to the producers.

"Please let them come and interview you," he said.

"Absolutely not. I am not going on that crazy show."

But I have to admit I was intrigued by the idea. I'd never really thought about being on television, and if I had, I probably would have seen myself on something like the *Charlie Rose Show*—pretty much the polar opposite of *Housewives*. When I'd bring up this outlandish idea to friends, I was surprised how many urged me to take it seriously. "It'll be fun." "What's there to lose?" "It will be good for your One Step Ahead initiative." "You can raise awareness for your charities." "It could lead to something bigger." And so on. I wasn't tempted, but I *was* curious. So when Jake pushed it, I agreed to an interview.

The producers came to our house. They filmed me nine months pregnant with Sienna, which was hilarious in and of itself. When I wasn't selected for the new season, I didn't care either way. Sienna was born, and Reid and I were thrilled. I was grinding my own organic baby food and breast-feeding around the clock. The thought of a film crew following me around was absurd. I had four kids and no idea how to juggle it all. I was starting to get overwhelmed (of course) about the avalanche of things to do.

When the older kids were in school, I took Sienna to one of my favorite restaurants, Via Quadronno on Seventy-third Street between Madison and Fifth, to meet a friend for lunch. Valerie Cooper was my mentor, a woman I looked up to and idolized. I said to her, "How am I going to do this? How can I get them all to school and make their meals? How am I going to read them all bedtime stories while nursing and help with homework?"

She smiled and said, "Just love them. When you feel overwhelmed, just love them."

It was the best advice I'd ever gotten. I'd been trying to do everything for each child, and that was what pushed me near the edge. Valerie's words gave me permission to be imperfect. I couldn't be with all of them at the same time. I couldn't do everything for all of them. But I could, and did, love them. I could hug and kiss them and make them feel cherished. If that was all I did, it would be enough.

So that was where my head was during the broadcast of season four. My days were packed with kid stuff, school and activities, homework and dinner. But I admit I did pay more attention to *Housewives*. Although I believed my joining the show was a dead issue, I still imagined myself among them. How would I react to this; what would I say about that. It was a fun little game I played with myself. A lot more fun, anyway, than imagining myself being interviewed by Charlie Rose.

The year went by in a blur. As crazy as it was, I remember that as a very happy year in our lives. I was in the Hamptons relaxing with the kids, watching a movie in the movie room when I received a phone call from Jen O'Connell, the executive producer of the show, saying that they would like to reconsider me for the next season's cast.

At my second *Real Housewives* interview, I looked more like myself. My pregnancy fuzziness had cleared up. I wasn't nauseated or green-skinned. My hair was clean, cut, and colored. They must have liked what they saw the second time around. A week later, they handed me a contract.

Deciding to be on this reality show was one of the hardest decisions of my life. Reid and I weren't so enthusiastic the first time around. But then we softened on the idea. It seemed, from the outside, like a fun adventure. But we had to think it through carefully. Reid and I had a lot to consider. The children, his business, our family and friends.

I still couldn't make up my mind. For a month, we went back and forth.

"Let's do it!" we agreed.

"No fucking way are we doing it!" we agreed.

"You have to do it," said Sarah and my half sister Michele.

"You'd be insane to do it," said other friends.

Fran Drescher said, "Break a leg—I mean that metaphorically. And lead with your philanthropy." As a philanthropist herself, she understood exactly why I wanted to do the show. If I could help just one person, it would be worth the risk.

My father was *way* into it. In the four years since Mom died, he'd been living it up in Miami. If he came on the show, he'd get attention (and dates) out of it.

I tended to agree with my friends who said I'd be insane to do the show, but being insane has never been a deal breaker for me. What concerned me most was that the Housewives didn't always come off so well. You could get the feeling that while they may put themselves forward as strong, confident people, they were really superficial. Their talk wasn't about current events or what they were reading or science or global crises; it was about parties, men, nail polish, clothes. Don't get me wrong, I can be all about parties, men, nail polish, and clothes. And certainly it wouldn't be a problem to fill forty-four minutes of that every week, but most of the time I'm that other person. I'm not saying I'm some deep brooding genius either, but this "real housewife" is somewhere in between. My greatest fear was losing control over how I was perceived. Maybe that's shallow in itself, but it doesn't only affect me; it can affect my family, now and in the future; it can affect the work I do for both a career and my charities. It also affects my self-image. I will absolutely cop to being shallow in that way.

But the reasons to say "yes" were far more practical. I was now in my forties with two degrees (including a law degree), four children, one husband, and no career. Being a real housewife and a real mom takes up all my time and gives me great satisfaction, but it's not enough. It can be mind-numbing. Being on a national primetime series could create opportunities. It wasn't lost on me that Bethenny Frankel used *Housewives* as a springboard to an industry that includes books, DVDs, products, and her own TV show.

And I would be getting a salary! It still allowed me to contribute to my family. Not enough to make any appreciable difference in how we lived, but earning money is good for the self-esteem, and it means my generous husband doesn't have to see my Botox bills.

You can see from the above that I wasn't completely altruistic in my consideration, but I did like that the show would give me a bully pulpit to advance awareness and acceptance of people with missing limbs. I wanted to show people that it was okay to be an amputee, that wearing a prosthesis was easy. I wanted to prove that amputees could do what everybody else could. When I was a girl and teenager, I didn't know any amputees. If I'd seen one on television who was married, had a couple of degrees, was a good mother to four children, ran around to lunches and parties in New York City, I would have felt better about myself and my future. It seemed like a door opener, a great opportunity.

The truth was, I still had one foot in the closet, as it were. Many of my friends, people I'd known for twenty years, were not aware that I wore a prosthesis. I hid and covered my leg as much at forty as I had at six. I wanted to take that final step of total exposure, which was a half step beyond total acceptance. I would expose myself for the sake of others. But I wanted an emotional breakthrough for myself, too.

"Reid, honey, do we have any skeletons in our closet here? Any extracurriculars I should know about?" I asked him one night.

"No!" he said. "Have you made any sex tapes, Aviva?" Nope. (Too bad. We would have become gazillionaires with a reality show *and* a sex tape. Oh well, you can't have it all.)

And finally, the most superficial reason of all—*television!* It may be a reality show, but it's still fun and a whole new experience. I'm not an exhibitionist, but remember me dancing on the tables in Alexandre's club? Well, that was me, too. It seemed cool that Perez Hilton would write lies about me; Page Six would get it all wrong; and I'd be getting a front-row seat and a back-stage pass to a phenomenal piece of pop culture.

In the shadow of these thoughts, I found myself moving away from "no." I believed our family life and marriage were strong enough to withstand the stress and publicity. I reckoned the novelty and celebrity the kids would enjoy would more than compensate for the inevitable teasing they might get at school. Jane might sue again or triple up on mediation appointments, but then again, Jane *always* might sue again.

Oh fuck it, let's do it.

All else aside, whatever would happen seemed very worth it in exchange for helping others on a really large scale.

My father always said, "Everything that you worry about never happens. But what you don't worry about does."

As a professional worrier, I spent a ton of time stressing out about the hundred things that *didn't* happen. The show didn't affect my husband, our marriage, his business, or our kids. Jane didn't sue. But I did get strung up by the press and the fans. It was all very new. Fran had warned me to have thick skin.

But I'm getting ahead of myself.

Reid and I signed the contract. As I prepared mentally and sartorially for filming, I took a long, hard look in the mirror. With four kids, I didn't have the time to do that too often. Oh, boy. I didn't love what I saw. The cameras would pick up every flaw and wrinkle, sag and bag. I had two months before shooting. That gave me just enough time to spruce up.

Surgery Number Seven and a Half: Bilateral Eyelid Lift

I went to one of the top plastic surgeons in Manhattan and said, "I'm kind of in a rush to have the procedure and heal before I start filming."

He said, "I can squeeze you in, but it'll have to be on August 20."

Naturally, because my lucky streak did not quit, that happened to be the day before Hurricane Irene, a monster storm that tore through New York, New Jersey, Connecticut, and New England, leaving massive devastation in its wake.

The doctor had a weekend house on Long Island. When I arrived at his surgical suite, he made it clear that he did not want to be there. He had to get to his house and batten down the hatches before the storm hit. So his frame of mind was nasty, and here I was with my five hundred questions. His patience with my anesthesia anxiety ran out by question number two. He refused to discuss it.

"I don't want general," I insisted. "Just numb the area around the eyes."

"We have to put you under. You can't handle it awake," he snapped.

"I had my leg cut off awake," I said, "I think I can handle an eyelift."

"An anesthesiologist will be in the room to put a catheter in your arm, just in case you can't deal with it," he said.

"It won't be necessary."

"I insist," said the doctor.

Reid squeezed my hand. He knew all this talk about anesthesia made me really anxious. This wasn't the proper state of mind to be in. "I'm telling you, I don't need it," I said, my voice cracking.

"Mr. Drescher, would you please leave the room?" asked the doctor.

Reid thought he was going to examine me, so he left. When the doctor and I were alone, he screamed, "Just stop making a big deal out of this! Let the system do its job! You're such a pain the ass!"

Oh, I *was* a pain in the ass. I had always *been* a pain in the ass. Doctors had been calling me one since I was six years old. But this was the first doctor who screamed in my face about it minutes before he was to take a knife to my eyes. He was angry, overbearing, and mean. Mussolini would have objected to this guy's bedside manner.

If I was anxious before, I was approaching meltdown now.

"I'm just really nervous," I said weakly. We were alone in the room. No Reid, no nurses. I was the last patient of the day. He just wanted to get out of there before the hurricane, which I sympathized with. But he didn't see how he'd save time if I had local anesthesia. It'd be faster, actually, considering recovery time. Not that I wanted the surgeon to rush. The very thought sent my anxiety through the roof.

I was cowed by his screaming, though, and kept quiet. I got on the table and was wheeled to the operating room. The anesthesiologist put the IV into my arm. I looked up at the doctor and asked, "Are you still angry?"

He said, "Yup."

"Are you going to be nice?"

"Nope."

And then he grabbed my head and injected my left eye with a local anesthetic. My eyelid blew up. I don't know if this is normal. All I know was my eye was glued shut, and a seriously pissed-off surgeon with a tray full of scalpels was hovering over me. With my open eye, I saw the furious look on his face. He could be the greatest plastic surgeon in the entire world, but that face was terrifying.

He came around to inject my other eye. I said, "Stop right there. I'm not doing this with you." I sat up.

He said, "All right. Let's call it a day."

He might've been relieved I saved him from himself. If he'd been angry during the surgery and made a mistake, his career would have been over.

I found Reid in the waiting room. He was completely cool and calm to see me with one huge swollen eye and no bandages ten minutes after being wheeled into surgery. The doctor told him we changed our minds. Reid asked, "Aviva, are you okay?"

"Let's get out of here," I said. I was kind of embarrassed, but relieved. For two weeks, I had one huge, swollen black eye. (Never got the surgery after all.)

The doctor shouldn't have bullied me, and he knew it. He gave us our money back.

One of the weirdest experiences of being on a television show in this era is that strangers can communicate with me through social media. At first, I was surprised by the hundreds of comments about me. When I did a good deed on camera, they were positive. When I created drama, they were negative. I was fascinated by the psychology of anonymous posters. Sometimes, I read the comments and smiled. Sometimes, I was hurt. Now I just laugh. I have become bulletproof. The plethora of opinions is simply one of the hazards of this profession.

I had a few conversations with Fran as well. She talked me down. Her ex-husband, Peter Jacobson, a TV producer and a creator of *The Nanny*, offered some hysterical, intelligent advice. "This is show *business*. Get it? *Business*. You should watch all of the old soap operas and become one of those characters," he said.

"What should I say when Ramona tells me my apology was disingenuous?"

He said, "Tell her, 'I always knew you were a smart woman, Ramona.'"

Peter had me on the floor laughing and reminded me not to take it too seriously, or seriously, at all.

Another Hollywood friend from high school, Jack Amiel, said, "Just remember the show and everything you do is just what happens between the commercials."

Early on, though, I was rattled by it.

After the reunions, the show was done. I resumed my ordinary life. I didn't regret doing the show. I wasn't happy that I appeared to dwell obsessively on my leg and my anxiety, though. Most of the people in my life had no idea about my fear of flying or panic attacks before the show aired. Since age eleven, I aspired to not make a big deal of it. That was my coping mechanism.

The show put my anxieties front and center. It seemed like I didn't talk or think about anything else. I'm obsessive about nonstick pans and health, but not in talking about my problems. It is my nature to put my leg and panic in the background in order to live to the fullest. That was my intention when I signed on to do the show.

I proved an amputee can do anything. During one of the last scenes of the season, I walked in a charity fashion show for Heather. She asked me to put a jacket on, and I decided to take it off at the last minute. I didn't mean to disrespect Heather or her undergarment line. It was a charity event, and I was glad she asked me to participate. What I thought was so funny about the negative fan reaction to "Jacketgate": no one asked, "What the hell is a forty-two-year-old woman with a fake leg doing on a runway in her underwear?"

The fact that I was exposing my leg—and my middle-aged body—didn't warrant a ripple of disapproval. That thrilled me. I'd succeeded at turning the attention away from my leg. No one cared a bit about it, or questioned my right to walk the runway. My behavior drew viewers' attention away from my leg. I got no special sympathy for it. They loved or hated me based only on who they perceived me to be. They forgot about my leg entirely.

Mission accomplished.

CHAPTER SIXTEEN

Lost and Found

A viva's not only lost her leg, she's lost her mind!"

That's pretty much the reaction I was expecting when I signed on to be a *Real Housewife of New York City*. Prime-time television is a sort of über-Facebook and my "status" would be out there—really, really out there. I assumed current friends and acquaintances would treat me as some kind of freak. Voices from the past would ring out with ridicule. And the response from the general public would be of the "real-housewife-my-ass-and-who-does-she-think-she-is" sort.

I couldn't have been more wrong. I've never experienced such an outpouring of warmth and support. Especially gratifying has been meeting so many amputees—children and adults—who seem to have gotten some strength and confidence from seeing me show my own condition.

Another exciting benefit has been the raised awareness and

increased contributions that have helped get prosthetics to more people in need. Even the acquaintances who didn't know about my prosthesis and friends who weren't aware of all my quirks responded with warmth and understanding. I'm very grateful to the *Real Housewives* world for giving me this forum.

Most of the letters from people from my past were pleasant surprises. One out-of-the-blue email via Facebook, though, really took me by surprise. I actually held my breath when I saw the address. Here it is, with permission:

Hi, Aviva. I've wanted to reach out for some time—decades even—I suppose in an effort to get a handle on an emotion that defies capture. Yet somehow the moment hasn't felt right. I really just want to say hello after all these years. Seize the day, as they say.

It has been a challenge just to slow life down for a minute to write you. Life seems to keep charging ahead regardless of how much I crave stillness. In the past month alone, a new job and a new house have taken up much spare time. I also have four children (ages 3–9), so "spare time" isn't quite the right term here, as you know.

This is all really just to say that I have been rooting for you all these years, and have been a champion in your corner, albeit invisible. Not many weeks have gone by when I haven't thought of you, wondered how you were, if our paths would ever cross, wondering how this experience of life was unfolding for you, and hoping for the very best for you. Here you are now with an incredible family, a loving supportive husband, a beautiful life, and of course an impeccable and enviable wardrobe.

I haven't seen the episode with your father, but my parents

watched it. They can't believe how fantastic he still is. "He was
always the most fun man in any room at any time," claims my
mom.

Well. So. Hello. After 35 years.

Much love, Rebecca

Becky Morgan! The girl who said, "It's a big deal," to ride the curve of the barn cleaner. The dare that changed my life—and hers.

So how big a deal was it? I don't claim it was tragic. But I'm not an idiot; it was huge. But huge in that abstract way that I know it must have been huge. I mean, I lost my bloody foot when I was six years old. I'm sorry, it just doesn't seem that big to me. It happened. I accepted it. I went on. Okay, I'll never be a prima ballerina (though I think I could kick ass on *Dancing with the Stars* if the whole *House-wives* thing doesn't work out). But I'll never be a violin virtuoso either.

Loss is a fact of life. Losing a leg isn't the worst loss in my life. As I reread these pages (to take out the stuff that could get me sued), I realized that I chronicled a number of losses, from the profound (my mother) to the serious (that limb) and the ordinary (lovers). I also noticed that there's a theme about how I felt about these losses: I came to terms with all of them. Not with forgiveness, because who am I to forgive? Not with forgetting, either. I'll never forget the people and history that are important to me. Not with closure, because I'm not even sure what that means. Not with "getting over it," because I'm not sure I can. I just made peace. I reached my kind of emotional settlements. Some were easier to accept than others, of course.

My Current's Ex. Mffft. Glbbt. Rsstd. You know, I still don't get it. What an enormous waste of time and money. Coming to terms with something doesn't mean you have to let go of all of your feelings—positive or negative. But I do have some understanding for Jane's feelings and aggressive behavior, and I'm not without sympathy. Most important, she's my oldest daughter's mother, and we're tied together in love and caring for Veronica. That's a very close bond. While there's still anger and regret, there's a whole lot that's beautiful.

My Dad's Guru. Okay, sorry, I'm not a saint. Neither was Sai Baba. And in whatever bizarre afterlife he may be enjoying himself in his celestial ripping off of the vulnerable, he can go fuck himself. That's the only term I'll come to with that whole thing.

My Ex. Making peace isn't like having a lobotomy where the offending part of the brain is removed. "Harry is a great guy"? Well, not entirely. I still love those parts of Harry and I love the son we have together. For me, Harry's faults are not obscured by his considerable charm. I don't think he's ever going to grow up, and that can be very irresistible in a man. As it turns out, it's not so much for me. In so many ways, Harry is a great guy. I wish my ex-husband, the father of my first-born, nothing but the best.

My Left Foot. If I had to do all over again, I'd keep you. Becky, I never blamed you for the accident. Forgiveness is not an issue. People usually grow apart from their childhood friends after they move away. Now I'm grateful you're back in my life.

That day changed both of our lives forever. We share it and how it affected us both.

My Angel. Mom, you were there for me when I needed you most. Now that I have children of my own, I can only imagine how horrible my accident was for you. That couldn't have helped the demons that pushed you to finding comfort in wine. I love you and think about you every day.

Love. That's how I came to terms with just about everything. So that's my life so far. It's a work in progress. Stay tuned.

Acknowledgments

It takes a village to get a book done and published! I've got a lot of people to thank.

Thanks Valerie Frankel, Judith Newman, Tricia Boczkowski, Jennifer Bergstrom, and Louise Burke for convincing me that I had an interesting story to tell. Thanks to Paul Schindler and Mark Merriman for your help. Transcriber Lynn Monty did fast and fabulous work typing my stories. Faren Bachelis did a wonderful job copyediting. Elisa Rivlin was very thorough. Thanks for asking me one hundred times, "Did that really happen?"

Thank you, Bravo and Andy Cohen, for this amazing opportunity and the platform to help amputees. By hiring me, so many physically challenged young, old, and new saw me on TV and had hope. Thank you, Shed Media, for putting in the meaningful scenes that made a difference. Your production team is stellar. Thank you, Jake Spitz and Bethenny Frankel, for the gig.

My *RHONYC* castmates! Thank you so much LuAnn, Ramona, Sonja, Carole, Heather, and Kristen for all the laughter, headaches, and silliness. You have been a pleasure to work with. We operate in a weird alternative universe few can understand.

The *RHONYC* viewers! Thank you! I love every minute of you. Your comments are awesome and the blogs are hysterical. You make the show so much fun to be a part of. I'm still amazed my life has taken this crazy turn, and that you've been there every step along the way.

ACKNOWLEDGMENTS

Thank you, Rebecca Morgan. Your kindness and support after all of these years has shown tremendous courage. I only wish thirty-five years had not gone by without you in my life.

Thanks, Dad, for giving me a great life filled with laughter and total craziness. Thanks for allowing me to scream. I love you.

Andre, Barbara, Michele, and Phil: You have been unconditionally giving and loving my entire life. I love you.

Dave, Adeline, Marilyn, Meryl, Stephen: Thank you for being in our lives. You bring our children tremendous joy. Here's to Ginjer—wherever you are—you were right.

Harry and Jane: Thank you for being wonderful parents.

Thank you, Jill Kargman, for believing in my writing and my story from Day One. You are the greatest well-wisher I know. Your cheering me on has been life changing. Your confidence, wit, and humor are awe-inspiring.

Thank you, Jennifer Gardner Trulson, not only for being a great friend but for making this book happen. You birthed it.

Thank you, Fran Drescher, for telling me to "lead with philanthropy" and for all your support. Thanks, Peter Jacobson, for making me laugh and helping me to understand a new and foreign world.

Thank you, Laura and Michael Cohen. You go above and beyond for our entire family. You are our family.

Sarah Levy, Stacey Griffith, Joanna Martowski, Dr. Ellen Marmur, Jackie Moffett, Melissa Breitbart Sohn, Matt Dillon, Anne Bowen, Scott Stackman (and others at CAFoundation), Alicia and Craig Gitlitz, Ileana Chu, Krissy and Alex Mashinsky, Mary Shepard, Philip Gorrivan, Nancy Leibowitz, Shoshana Halpern, Rosie Pope, Susan Baker, Thomas Roberts, Patrick Abner, Sara Pilot, Dr. Bernard Kruger, and Wendy Madden: Where would any of us be without the love and support of good friends? Thank you all.

ACKNOWLEDGMENTS

Thank you, Amy Winters and Erik Schaffer and everyone at One Step Ahead Foundation. You go above and beyond.

Most importantly, I'm eternally grateful for my family. Reid, you have shown me what love truly is. You continue to sweep me off my feet in the most profound way. You are the most incredible father to Harrison, Veronica, Hudson, and Sienna. Thank you for leading them by example.

Harrison, Veronica, Hudson, and Sienna: You are the reason I wake, breathe, work, write, and give. You make every minute I live worth living. Watching you grow into beautiful little people brings me the most incredible joy. You don't know it, but you sacrificed to make this book happen. Thank you. I love you more than life.

Lastly, to all my friends who've lost limbs: Each and every day, you remind me of the strength of the human spirit. You inspire me. Thank you so much.

Printed in the United States
By Bookmasters